Visualization

The Best Creative Visualization
Techniques

*(How Successful People Use the Power of
Manifesting and Subconscious Brain to Achieve
Goals)*

Mattie Rossiter

Published By **Zoe Lawson**

Mattie Rossiter

All Rights Reserved

Visualization: The Best Creative Visualization Techniques (How Successful People Use the Power of Manifesting and Subconscious Brain to Achieve Goals)

ISBN 978-1-77485-575-1

No part of this guidebook shall be reproduced in any form without permission in writing from the publisher except in the case of brief quotations embodied in critical articles or reviews.

Legal & Disclaimer

The information contained in this ebook is not designed to replace or take the place of any form of medicine or professional medical advice. The information in this ebook has been provided for educational & entertainment purposes only.

The information contained in this book has been compiled from sources deemed reliable, and it is accurate to the best of the Author's knowledge; however, the Author cannot guarantee its accuracy and validity and cannot be held liable for any errors or omissions. Changes are periodically made to this book. You must consult your doctor or get professional medical advice before using any of the suggested remedies, techniques, or information in this book.

Upon using the information contained in this book, you agree to hold harmless the Author from and against any damages, costs, and expenses, including any legal fees potentially resulting from the application of any of the information provided by this guide. This disclaimer applies to any damages or injury caused by the use and application, whether directly or indirectly, of any advice or information presented, whether for breach of contract, tort, negligence, personal injury, criminal intent, or under any other cause of action.

You agree to accept all risks of using the information presented inside this book. You need to consult a professional medical practitioner in order to ensure you are both able and healthy enough to participate in this program.

Table of Contents

Chapter 1: The Way To Make The Universe Listen 1

Chapter 2: Focusing Utilizing Visualization 9

Chapter 3: Passions And Desires 14

Chapter 4: Gift Self The Gift Of Clarity.... 20

Chapter 5: Cultivating Createive Dreams 35

Chapter 6: Create Your Dream Life 44

Chapter 7: The Way Our Brains Function 49

Chapter 8: What Are The Benefits Of Lucid Dreaming? 63

Chapter 9: Illustrations To Prosperity, Wealth And The Pursuit Of Success 72

Chapter 10: Control Your Emotions To Be Happier 85

Chapter 11: Law Of Attraction 101 What Is It And How It Functions.......................... 99

Chapter 12:10 Fantastic Tips For Greater Concentration And Focus 103

Chapter 13: The Laws Of Attraction, Polarity And Negative Beliefs 109

Chapter 14: Grounding To Support Meditation And Visualization 116

Chapter 15: Tips To Increase Your Creativity 127

Chapter 16: Prevention Of Self-Consciousness Excessive 141

Chapter 17: Procrastination Stagnation, And Personal Growth: 146

Chapter 18: Why The Mind Work Like It Does 155

Chapter 19: Over-Thinking Can Be A Numbing 167

Chapter 20: Practicing Creative Visualization 174

Chapter 1: The Way To Make The Universe Listen

Do I have the ability to have whatever I want simply by contemplating it? If that's the case then why don't we billionaires?

One of the main reasons this law does not affect certain people is that their vibrations aren't enough to achieve their goals. The inability that the law works to accomplish its magic is usually due to an unbalanced state of mind between the conscious and subconscious mind. To allow dreams to manifest each cell of your body must be vibrating at with the identical frequency. Every single part of you needs to request the universe to do exactly the same thing. In the absence of this, there will be an internal conflict. An internal struggle of wills in a way. This blurry message confuses universe, which usually responds in a similar way. In other words, if transmit to the universe a misguided message, you will receive a chaotic life.

Check out this example:
If you ask for a promotion, but your subconscious mind insists that it's too tough and you'll never

receive a promotion, you're likely to not be promoted.

How do I sync my subconscious and conscious minds?

This is achieved by the process of goal setting, visualization, and affirmations. Be aware that even though it's your conscious mind which makes the decision, it is your subconscious mind that is responsible for the execution of your decision. If you set goals, you imagine your goal coming true and affirm it often Both the rational and the imaginative parts in your brains are engaged. What can an affirmation be? Affirmations are when you are in control of your mind by making simple, positive, and powerful declarations. They reinforce our belief about the possibilities of the action we want to take.

Here are some affirmations that are positive:
"I am a magnet for money I am a money magnet, and money comes easily"
"I am healthy and content and have a wonderful relationship with my kids"

What's the trick to achieving these objectives?

With the practice of using positivity and affirmations on a regular basis to get the things we want.

The subconscious brain is extremely difficult to change, however it is possible to reprogram it with affirmations and subliminal messages which will be covered in the subsequent chapters.

I've tried affirmations in the past. Why is it that the universe didn't listen to me at the time?

Every time you imagine something, or experience something or feel it, your universe gets it and interprets it. The universe takes that as your intent.

In the beginning, you must be clear about your motives. Like we said that sending multiple messages to the universe can give you an unanswerable response at the best. When writing letters to a person of importance it is important to be cautious about the language of your demands. The message must be precise. In addition, you need to take it seriously. It must be true to your highest desires. If your request doesn't sound convincing enough then the universe is likely to refuse your request.

If you want to be successful and you want to achieve it, then build a picture of success. Think about what success is to you. Set your goals in order and then prioritize them.

Example:
Do not just seek out an ideal soulmate. Give the universe the exact details of what you'd like for the soulmate of your dreams. What are the most important qualities of your soulmate? What are the characteristics you share? What are the interests you have in common? What are the activities you would like to do with each other?

Examples of properly phrased intents are:
I'd like to find to meet a man who is as much about the environment like I do.
I'd like to meet a woman who like me is obsessed with art.

Once you've established your goal You must enhance the effectiveness of your goal. This could be accomplished by visualization that will be explained in depth in the subsequent chapters. Keep in mind that to make visualizations work it is necessary to be able to see the sensation, feel it and hear the goal with such vivid clarity within your mind's senses that you could almost sense, feel, and taste and hear it through the physical features of your body.

In the next step, you must rid your energy storage. To allow the message to get through you must clear the channel through which it is carried. What blocks these channels? Negative energy. It manifests in the form in the form of thoughts that are negative. This is the voice of fixed thinking in behind your head telling you: "You don't deserve it. Therefore, you shouldn't get the thing." Oder "Maybe you're entitled to it. But since life isn't fair and you're not going to get it."

The process of clearing your energy reserves is about squelching that voice with a strong embedded which allows the positive mind voice to be heard.

The most effective methods for getting rid of negative energy are yoga and meditation.

All of these are ineffective unless you expect that you will receive a response by the Universe.

When you send your email address to someone you're hoping for that they will receive the message. In addition, you want that they will respond. Therefore, you check your email periodically. When you place an order for pizza and wait for the delivery driver to arrive at your door. You make the precise amount. You could even place a few beer in your freezer, and take down the table in order to make room for pizza.

It is essential to adopt the same mindset when you send an inquiry towards the Universe.

If you've have asked the universe for the birth of a child and you're waiting for it to arrive, you must anticipate the arrival of the baby. Do your best to live as if that the baby will be coming soon. This means that you save funds to support the baby. The mom of the future should take a balanced diet in order to ensure her body is ready for her baby. Check out your home. Do you see enough space for a baby? It doesn't mean that you need to purchase a larger house or spend a lot of money on infant clothes, particularly when you don't have the funds to purchase it. It's actually the smaller items that matter, like removing your home of clutter to make it suitable for children. Sometimes, you have to make changes to your lifestyle. Do you live your lives as the responsible parents you'll soon be? It might be time to go slow on your drinking. Be the person you are telling the universe that yes we're ready for the birth of a child.

Another thing be aware of when you are communicating with your universe, is the energy you produce will be wasted if you don't direct it in the right direction. It's not enough to simply declare that you want to make the necessary actions towards your objectives. For example, you are constantly praying to the universe for an ongoing relationship with a good person. Yet, you continue meeting emotionally unresponsive people. You continue to ask for the universe to help you become successful. If you don't dress to be successful, then don't be expecting it to happen. Also, you must act as if your dreams have already been realized. This means getting the most of the gifts that the universe has offered you.

Be patient, too. Be aware that the concept of time is not applicable for the entire universe. What to you may appear to be forever could be nothing more than a glance in another realm. If your money, your partner in crime or whatever it is that you've prayed to the universe to bring you hasn't come yet, don't despair. Know that it will require time as the environment must work and blend together to meet your desires.

It is better to be alert for opportunities. The universe sometimes responds to your requests in unexpected ways. Be alert for opportunities or the universe's answer could slip without notice.

If you'd like your life to be different you can't do it when you do the same thing have been doing for a long time.

Chapter 2: Focusing Utilizing Visualization

Visualization is a technique of continuously imagining the desired result so that the individual can increase the likelihood of getting it. This is another technique you can employ to improve your ability to concentrate.

The most effective method to use visualization is not to imagine the final result. Instead, you should imagine the "process" that will reach the desired outcome.

This is based on a psychological and social study that was conducted by three students. One group was asked to imagine them passing an exam. Another group was instructed to imagine their preparation for the test. The third group did not receive any instruction to imagine.

The results revealed that those who had a mental image of themselves passing not perform as well as the two other groups, however, those who imagined themselves in a classroom showed higher results than the other two groups.

Visualization: How to Increase Focus
Traditional visualization requires you to visualize the end goal, whereas modern visualization

encourages you to imagine the process before reaching the ultimate goal. The best results can be obtained out of both by visualizing the process and the final outcome.

To increase your concentration on one goal Visualize the goal as clearly as you can. For instance, if your goal is to get fit , then imagine you looking strong, fit and fit. Imagine you looking great in that garment you've always wanted to wear, but you feel you're not able to.

Apart from that you could also imagine your body eating healthier food such as whole food items and green juice, running early in the morning , taking a workout after your work hours, as well as other visualisations of the activities you are sure will help you achieve your goal.

Visualizing every step you have to complete, your mind can be focused on working towards your final goal. Through visualizing your goals you feel motivated to keep working toward it.

Be aware that visualization isn't only a once-in-a-lifetime exercise. Like all exercises that increase your concentration it is recommended to do this regularly.

Tips on how to perform Visualization
It is not necessary to complete all the steps in one

go. It is recommended to gradually improve your daily visualization to get it as thorough as you can. The steps are split into three phases to assist you in making use of visualization slowly and efficiently.

First Stage
Step 1: Sit down in a cool and quiet location. Spend some time relaxing and enjoy a good mood. Eliminate any distractions, like your cell phone. While you're focused on visualizing, it's essential to avoid being disturbed.
Step 2. Relax your eyes, and draw the mental picture of the goal. Relax your body and breathe deeply while you create the picture.
Step 3: Gradually include more details in your image, including the physical location in which you have achieved your goal and how you feel when you have succeeded. Imagine yourself in the first person. One method to help you accomplish this is to simply open your eyes and taking a look at your hands with complete concentration before closing your eyes. Now, you can begin to picture yourself as the person you are within your mental picture.

Second Stage

Step 1: Relax in your favorite corner and shut your eyes. Replay the mental picture you created in Steps 1 & 2 as accurately you can. You'll know if you're 100% focused when you are easily capable of recalling your mental picture.

Step 2: Create "flashbacks" about how you managed to accomplish your objective. Start with the initial step, which could be right where you are in the moment. Continue to the next three and the next. Think of it as a list of the steps.

Step 3 3. Visualize the steps detail. Imagine yourself performing the first step and then completing the second step. Continue to follow it

Third Stage

Step 1: Relax in a quiet spot and shut your eyes. Imagine the mental images you created in the previous step in as detailed as you can. Think about it from beginning to end.

Second step: Implement adjustments when necessary. For example, if you find that there obstacles that hinder you from completing goals you have set Imagine how you could deal with them and remain in the right direction.

Use visualization every day to help you stay focused on the things you must do. By doing this, you will keep you motivated and focused. It's good to know that many who engage in regular visualization say it has helped them build confidence in themselves and boost their mood.

Chapter 3: Passions And Desires

The functions of a human heart are to swim in deep waters However, someone with an understanding of them can draw these waters away (Proverbs 20:5)

Every action we take, there has to be a rationale behind the action. Sometimes it's represented by the basic motives behind our lives, but at or there may be moral or selfish motives behind our actions, as well as the inherent reactions that result from them, or. However, we all can acknowledge that everything we do, as well as all that we talk about, originates from a particular desire. Perhaps it's the urge to eat delicious and juicy hamburgers or the pleasure of helping peers in society, you're enticed by it. You're looking for it, but frequently, you don't know that you want it, and you lose sight of what it is that you want and where it came from and what it's headed towards.

Desires are the beginning of your life story. Without a specific motivation or desire and a passion, you won't be able to start your path and path to your ultimate ambition. What is the reason you would like to be a part of the world?

Because you are in love with it. however, one must figure the true meaning of what you want to do and important for your life, and as well as the lives of others, and whether it's in line with God's will. The God's plan as we saw in the previous chapter is to make us happy.

This chapter will discuss the difference between real and false dreams and ways to be able to discern from each other and get back the power of your own personal story. Let's sort between the both, will we?

Living a life of thought is following God's guidelines and leading an enjoyable life. However, in the modern world, times, challenges could appear.

They are deceiving and extremely difficult to overcome. A lot of false hopes cause procrastination and apathy. Schopenhauer is a nineteenth century German philosopher who was of the view that all human suffering and mishaps result from two distinct causes, principally boredom and pain which are the two primary negatives of happiness, as his views were.

To be apathetic is obviously, to commit sin and led astray. When we think our happiness and stability depend on external factors instead of internal ones we are prone to alternating between boredom and pain. Humans, being rational beings created with the gift of God strive to constantly stay away from pain and seek comfort, which is why we become bored. When we get bored, we then begin to fight with this sensation and pursue potentially hazardous activities that produce new types of stress that engulf our minds, causing harm to us. For instance, due to boredness, people may gamble and risk more than they can afford and hurt themselves and their families or others may participate in certain sports that cause injury to themselves without the commitment and skills that are essential for the practice of that particular type of sport. To prevent or overcome the aforementioned circumstances, we must be aware of our self-control and be aware about our choices.

Every time a desire that is common arises in your mind take a moment to think about it and envision the result. Do you stand to gain from it? Or will it cause more harm than positive? Why are you compelled to take this or that action? Are you motivated because you feel it or do you desire an instant reward or appraisal?

Imagine yourself as an circle. In the vicinity, there are spheres , which gravitate toward you in varying degrees. You are the most powerful planet, and you have the most powerful magnetic field. You decide what should attract you, and you do not want to gravitate around. Imagine this as a sphere inside you, and then try to imagine your rational thinking and will as the central point of this circle. Then try to picture your desires in the same way as the other spheres which are slowly trying to enter your field of gravitation. Are you willing to let them circle around your body? Are you willing to let your light shine upon these desires just as the light of Sun shines upon the Earth or the light of God over all humanity? Do not forget that once you allow these desires orbit your body, they will trigger the reaction that is evident externally.

The reason I came up with the exercise above is to remind you of your own flawed psyche which, in line with what we talked about just a few paragraphs ago to separate your wheat and shreds. You might find that doing this carefully and with confidence will allow you to escape the nasty effects of boredom and procrastination and can be an enormous boost to your happiness as well as your general life.

The strong desires are rewarded with powerful results. The manifestation of strong desires occurs over a longer time, unlike false ones that are connected to instant sensation of satisfaction, and are rooted solely in the world of the material. For instance, the desire to contribute to your community, or to take care of your family or be content. If you pursue your passions properly, will reap of their benefits and improve your life and that of those that surround you. Every one of these is in line with long-term spiritual and physical outcomes and is also in line with the Lord's desire of His own creations.

Hope and love are the underlying factors that infuse every of us with God's love and it's our job to cultivate and cultivate these feelings to God's glory. What is the best way to do with our lives? Should we be fighting over minor differences that are rooted in the sinful flesh of this world, or live a contemplative life in which we aim to improve our self every day, with higher thinking, and driven by the sole goal of achieving the Will of God? Are we going to choose to tell an unhappy story of our lives, or do we choose to write happy ones in which everyone are able to prosper and enjoy what we have gathered from our and efforts? If you think every day about what you are able to do the best today it is possible to enrich your life and make the most out of it. Let's continue.

Chapter 4: Gift Self The Gift Of Clarity

In the beginning chapter, you've made the decision to take charge of your own happiness. Congratulations. I've also guided you through the steps of editing your life and make the best option for personal improvement.

This chapter you'll have begin working on your memories from the past. The events of your past create a shadow over your life. They can make you feel inadequate. They can take away an enormous amount of energy and energy as there are many unresolved problems.

It's possible that you're unhappy, grieving or your self-esteem may have been shattered. You might feel like you're not enough, too ugly or not worthy of being loved. Whatever conclusion you draw from your experiences this is keeping you from moving forward and pulling you back from the life of success you could be living.

This chapter we'll try examine the facts you thought were truthful. It could be that your past experiences could not be the way you believe they are.

In actual fact there has been numerous research studies that have shown that people inflate or exaggerate certain memories from the past. This shouldn't come as an issue. People who believe the memories of their children are reliable give themselves too much credit.

There's a reason eyewitness testimony isn't the most effective way to prove a case in the courts of law. There are people who have inaccurate memories. It is possible that people are viewing an event from a perspective which may not provide an accurate picture of what actually happened. They might be thinking overly far.

Whatever the circumstance whatever the case may be, there's the reason that courts across all of the United States rigorously test eyewitness testimony. It's not as it's made out to be.

This is also true for your memory. It is possible that your memory is sporadic. It could be that you can only recall one specific detail, however there are numerous other details missing that are vital to accurately interpret that crucial detail you hold onto. It could be that your memories are distorted specifics.

Everyone agrees that these events occurred however the issue is that you're focusing too much on just a few particulars that you've blown them to the point of being ridiculous and created a lot of opportunity to interpret your memories in a negative manner.
Similar to your memories, they could appear to be a mix of different memories. However, when you look about the past, it's like them were one single memory. This is a huge problem because when things occur during the course of time, they take place in various circumstances. These contexts can have a significant influence on what the memories refer to.

In the end, you might not have any memory in the first place. It could be that you're only recollecting a small part of the story that is based on a fact and everything else is an interpretation. When you think of your past experiences, it's recalling the emotional state of your mind or recall of the event in the context of what you've interpreted.

If you're experiencing one or more of these, your memories might not be what you believe they are. You could be fighting with yourself emotionally about things that cause you to feel uneasy. They may not be grounded in the reality. They could not be happening at all for the major part.

The best way to Escape the past's grip on Your Life

In order to let go, you have to follow the following steps. These steps will allow you to get rid of the grip of the way that you decide to look at your past.

Remember that you are the editor of your life. Also, you are accountable for your personal life. Accept the responsibility of answering these questions. Be honest and you'll be able to be free of your suffocating memories and let them go.

What are the "Facts" Are they really facts?

There is no doubt that when someone uses the term "fact," they mean something particular. They refer to things that actually took place. They're not disputed. There's no reason to argue.

Did one car crash into another vehicle? Did the dog be run over by a vehicle? Is the person alive? Did this person pass away from malignancy or something else?

They are simply statements of truth that are in black and white. You must consider: Are the information I'm recalling actually facts according to the classical meaning of this word?

How can you accomplish this? First, you must ask who you are, what is and where, as well as when, what's the reason and what. You must ask these questions.

In this way you dissect the information you think are facts. It could be an interpretation. It could be a person's opinion. It could be a mix of comments from other people. It could also be an emotional reaction to an incident that occurred.

When you ask these kinds of questions and you are able to recollect the actual events.

Be sure to ask "Why" Then, make sure you ask "Why"

If you're asking questions like who, what and where how, and why, leave the topic about "why" up to the end. No matter what you're doing don't inquire "why" at first. It's a way to undermine yourself if do this.

Be sure to focus initially on other issues. You can examine the events you believe occurred in the past, and it could turn out that there are a few gaps in your memories. The truth is that some events didn't go as planned you imagined.

Then, look for evidence to back up your claims. Do you have any objective evidence that you can use to confirm that these events really occurred or were performed in the manner you remember them?

It is vital. Are there any people you could speak to who went through the same experience like you? Did they experience the same thing you did? Did they understand what you were saying?

Request confirmation. Don't assume just because it was uncomfortable and you felt embarrassed and degraded that it really happened according to the way you imagine it did. Find a new pair of eyes or an additional set of ears. This can make a significant difference.

Another thing to think about is whether the things you think about are consistent throughout time. Do you have the same events happening 10 years ago, as similar to what happened five years ago, or as similar as they are the present?

Be wary when memories you hold in your mind change with time. It could be more due to your attitudes and events you experienced than the actual events that took place.

When you've posed these tough questions to yourself you should be able to make transparent whether you're bad "memories" are grounded in fact or not. If not then your task is easy and that is to Let them go. It's that simple.

If your memories aren't founded on fact take them off your mind. They're not going to make you feel unsatisfied right now. They don't have any business influencing or altering how you feel about others and your feelings about yourself, or what you think about the future.

Don't hold them on because they're not based on actual facts. The longer you hold in to these beliefs, the further likely you will make yourself appear to be lying. You're doing yourself a disservice by beating yourself up.

Are There Facts Missing?

The next step you must include an internal analysis of the consistency as well as the quality of your negative memories.

Are there parts missing? You might remember one important element, but in order for the details to give you the meaning that you've got it, there have to be additional elements. There must be additional specifics.

Did you complete them? If so, did opt to fill them with the most shaky assumptions? If yes then can you remove those pieces that are negative and substitute the pieces with something positive or at a minimum neutral?

For instance, you go into a gathering and some very attractive ladies started laughing at your direction. It's easy to assume that you're unattractive and socially awkward, or otherwise not attractive to these women. They're so gorgeous that you felt intimidated by them.

What's the issue here? It's not like you leapt into conclusions. You only knew that they were looking in you in the direction of your gaze and were laughing. This is where your memories start and end. This has brought you to conclude that you're in somehow, not attractive.

So what's the impact? It's less likely that you'll be able to meet those of the opposite sexe nowadays. This is especially true when the woman is extremely, beautiful.

Here's the problem. If you look back at that memory, it could be due to someone laughing behind you. Maybe you were in the room along with other individuals and there was some sort of joking around in the back. It might be that the gorgeous women you believed were laughing at are actually playing with the man who was behind you.

It's not a big deal to interpret your memory this way, because there are pieces missing. Why are you forced try to cover up the gaps in your memory using the most flimsiest "facts" you can come across?

The most damaging "fact" in this case is they're in a state of laughter. It's an assumption. It is your responsibility for filling in the gaps by using, at a minimum either something positive or at the very least it's something neutral.

The final word? If your memories of the past are merely corrosive compilations of constructed details, consider questioning the corrosive information. Replace them with something neutral and then go through the memory once more.

If it is logically logical after filling the gaps with positive or neutral facts, let the memory go. Do you understand the way this plays out?

Be aware that there could be missing parts in your memories. Don't get yourself into a bind by constantly thinking that the most destructive as well as negative reasons are the ones that are the most "realistic" explanations.

Could your past experiences be read in a different manner?

If you are faced with the details of a moment that haunts you deeply Do you focus on the emotional effect? Do you focus solely on how embarrassed, humiliated and ashamed you were then or how you feel today?
Do you only focus on your anger, rage and the need to revenge? Do you dwell on how hurtful it is to be removed from the person you love?

Remove your attention from your emotions. Instead, consider the facts in the most objective way feasible. I am sure this is difficult but you have to take the initiative.

Imagine that you're someone other. Make it appear as if you're a kind alien being from another planet , and you are watching how these events unfold within your daily life.

From this perspective you can ask yourself Do you think there is only one method to understand these facts? Answer truthfully.

All else being all things being equal, there's a

good possibility you "negative memory" could be read in a positive manner. If not, it's possible to interpret it in a neutral manner. If that's the case, then you need to question your memory.

Tell you, "I've been interpreting this in the most sloppy way. I'm seeing this in a manner that angers me and hurts me. It also creates a feeling of a bitter person. It happened quite a while ago. I think it's time to see it in an unbiased manner."

You should focus on the phrasereal. This should awaken you. It's not realistic to interpret things in the most demeaning way that is possible. You're doing yourself no favors.

Try to view the memory more positive or at a minimum, an impartial way. If you're able to accomplish this, repeat it until you're able to let it go.

If your traumatizing past is based on actual facts and not an incorrect interpretation or "filling the gaps" you can assert your rights to live the life you want.

Here's the final scenario. If you examine your

memory and find it to be based upon facts that you're not conjuring up out of thin air. It's not like you're filling in the gaps by using the most flimsiest of details. You're not looking at the events in the most negative way that is possible.

The truth is that they happened, and were extremely brutal. Perhaps you were sexually assaulted. Perhaps your mother tried to kill you. Perhaps somebody tried to stabbing you.

They are extremely painful however, I urge to ask you to pause and say to yourself: Do I want allow these painful memories to hold grip over me throughout my life? This has happened sometime in the past. It's not something I can do about it.

There's no device that allows me to travel through time to reverse things. The events occurred as I remembered these events. They are real however I love myself far enough to allow these experiences ruin and devalue my life.

Create your own ideas But the final outcome will be the same. Clean your life. Be responsible for your happiness today. Nobody else will do it for you.

Everyone talks about how they are complete and how much they love you but in the final analysis, everyone's required to look after themselves. Everyone has enough challenges of their own, which is why you need to take charge.

Do not wait around for another person to fix your issues for you. They're not likely to be there, and when they do but they're not likely to give 100 100%.

You must do it. Make your way to your dream life today. Let go. It's not an easy task. It's not likely to be done in a day But you have to be persistent.

It is essential to continue chipping on these fantastical memories. They may be based on actual facts however, that doesn't disqualify you from the responsibility to yourself.

You have to take control of your life now. It is time to take control of your present life. It's true that the past may not belong to you However, you know what? It doesn't matter.

You control the way you respond to these facts in the present. React with self-control and life-ownership. Take control of your actions.

The more you practice this and the more you do it, you will recognize that you possess enormous power. You are able to take control of the past, allowing you to have an improved present that will help you build an optimistic future.

It's possible that this doesn't unfold in a way that is dramatic but it doesn't have to. If you're able notice certain changes when you take control of your life and life-control, be proud of your power. Be grateful that you control your life.

Chapter 5: Cultiveating Createive Dreams

The initial step to achieving the goal of anything is a desire. This desire should not be flimsy. It needs to be concrete. If you really want something that is consuming, it will consume your mind your body, soul and even your body. It will always be in your thoughts. A desire to eat a pizza may be a wish but it's only a temporary one. It will not remain in your mind for a long time.

Everyone has laughed at the humor of a Jim Carrey film at some moment. However, when he was only fifteen, the actor quit high school to help his musician father. At the time his family was in the lower middle-class, but they soon fell to the bottom of the pile. In the end the family were homeless. They slept in an unoccupied van. But he refused to let his burden drag him down. His father took him to their "house" to the most part, to comedy clubs on and off until his hopes were realized and he was among the most popular comics of his time.

The author Stephen King is quite famous for his books that have recently been made into highly popular films. However, when Stephen King first began to realize his goal the first novel he wrote was rejected by thirty publishers. He had his vision in the back of his mind however, it was rejected by publishers across the world including King for a brief amount of time. The pressure of not being successful hinder his objectives. With the support of his wife, he pushed on. He didn't let rejection stand in his way. He completed his novel and his novels have sold more than 350 million copies.

The rapper Jay-Z was born in the most ideal areas in Brooklyn However, he knew at an early age that he was going to become an established artist. The record labels were not willing to accept him, even though. Nobody believed in his visions, aside from him. What did He did? He came up with his own label that has become extremely lucrative and has brought an estimated fortune of $500,000.

A few years ago, surfer Bethany Hamilton lost her arm during an attack by sharks. She was just 13 when she suffered a loss of her left arm but a month later she returned on her surf board , and two years later she took home the first place at the NSSA National Championships. There was nothing that could stop her from achieving her goal and not even losing her arm. In the case of Bethany There was not a Plan B. The only option was Plan A.

Anyone who has watched E.T., Jurassic Park and Jaws are familiar with the ever-popular Steven Spielberg. The now famous filmmaker was disqualified from USC's film program twice. He didn't go and continued to pursue his goals. Today , he holds an honorary degree and serves as an official trustee of the University.

Recall the stories in the introduction. The man who wanted only to leave the neighborhood and attend college didn't let anything get between him and his goal. The man who needed to find an employment opportunity to ensure his family's survival was not letting small mistakes hinder him from achieving his goal. There was no other option. There was no backup plan in the event that plan A didn't work. There was only one option and they'd never stop until they had achieved plan A.

To truly experience success, it is essential to not make a plan B. There is no turning back. There is only one option. You must make it clear that your sole option is to take a step forward and help make your goals become reality. A burning desire to reach success, and win, is vitally important.

Without it, you'll never succeed in your goals. Anyone who is educated about money, is interested in it. They're always looking for more of it constantly. But asking to have money as everybody can testify is not going to result in it happening. Nearly every child has heard at some point or other that "money does not grow on trees". If someone is driven by a desire to be rich and a burning need for more money, this mindset can turn into an obsession. That being said take a look at these things:

First: Be definite. In terms of psychologically, you'll be more at achieving your financial goals if have a clear amount of money on your list. We'll get into more detail about this in the future.

Second: Decide the amount you're willing offer in exchange for the money you need. Many people believe that it is not free to give anything away. You'll have to contribute something , whether it's your time, physical work painting that you made or even a piece of art, etc. ....

Third: Create a deadline. This is the date at which you'll need your exact quantity of funds.

Fourth: Create your plan and outline the steps you will take to achieve this objective.

Fifth Five: Write it down. Note it down and then post it somewhere where you will easily see it.

This can lead towards...

Sixth: Go through your essay every day. Put it in a place where you are likely to see it every day. For some, it's their workplace. Others prefer the mirror in the bathroom. Wherever it is you are, it is important to regularly check it out to keep the goals at the forefront of your head.

It is crucial to adhere to all six steps.

Be sure to let go from all thoughts of "impossible" to instead develop an interest in going that's equivalent to taking the leap.

It is your responsibility to convince yourself that you can achieve your dream of creativity before it becomes a reality. Keep in mind that to complete these steps, you don't have to be from a specific background or have an academic level that is certain. It is not necessary to give up or put in the effort to get started with these steps. You must cultivate an interest and a strategy, and finally believe you can accomplish your goal. If you don't visualize those two million dollars that you can imagine in your head and you don't have it in your savings account.

To transform your dream into something tangible, you have to be able to define a reason or a strategy. It is important to be patient to be able to dream. You shouldn't be scared of the new or different things. Don't let other people's opinions influence your decisions.

If you're trying to save up for Italy and someone insists that there is "no way" that you'll succeed in making your money on time, you should stop talking about it. Don't listen to them , and do not let their negative thoughts hinder you believing that it can occur, and then creating the conditions for it to happen.

Every major achievement in the history of mankind was the result of a single dream. Every major breakthrough or new development in technology, every medical breakthrough, all started by a desire. Therefore, don't be scared to think about your goals. Don't let the world keep you from being kind and open-minded.

People might not like you for having dreams or claim that you're being unpractical. Do not let their opinions hinder you from achieving your goals. Instead, find the strength to continue to work hard and not to be influenced by them. Keep smiling and making them question why you are so enthusiastic.

Before reading your next chapter ensure that your thoughts are filled with the courage, tolerance and hope.

There's a vast distinction between wanting

something and actually being able to accept it. If you want to be successful however, you're not a person of patience and determination, and aren't ready to put in the effort required to attain this success, you'll continue to dream of prosperity instead of actually having them. There is no way to accomplish something they aren't sure they can accomplish. Your mindset is the key for your achievement.

The actor who is now famous who was only looking to be on television for all his life. He was aware of this from the very beginning. He took an old bus to the town next door each week, so that he could be a part of their community theater group as his town did not have a program. He kept doing this for long enough until he decided to relocate towards Los Angeles. As with many other stories, he boarded onto a bus using an one-way ticket as well as the shirt that was on his back. He tried to audition for the job repeatedly. He barely managed to get by, and over time, there was no call to return. But he didn't allow that to stop him. He spent his last cent on food before going to an audition for a part in a sitcom comedy, as a poor, ineffective actor. He was eventually offered the role, which was his first film role and, after filming the pilot, he used his earnings to purchase the first meal he had eaten for months.

He didn't stop. He knew what his goal was and knew that the achievement of it was more important than anything else. He was aware that he would require some stage experience which is why he traveled in his youth to gain every opportunity to gain experience. He was aware that he'd have to keep auditioning to be able to get an audition which is why he spent every minute of his time doing it.

He was never one to accept the idea of failure or poverty. He didn't let his endless defeats convince him that was not enough or that this wasn't the way he wanted to be. He was never discouraged. This is what you need to achieve your goals. It is impossible to accept defeat. It is essential to remain committed to that passion within you and never give up in your pursuit of your goals. If you're emotionally incapable of accepting anything less than the success you desire, then you're mentally ready to realize your goals and be successful.

Chapter 6: Create Your Dream Life

I would wake every day wanting to be completely free of all the things in my life. I was constantly of what I did not have. This was causing me to be anxious and scared which is why I was attracted to more people who were similar to me. I was tired of being like this. I wanted to know the key to feeling happy every day since I heard it from people such as Tony Robbins that success without fulfillment is not a success. I wanted to know how I could get rid of these negative feeling from my life and be happy right now. In the last six months, I finally figured out the things I've always long wanted to know about my entire life.

I was able to understand how the law of attraction works, and If you can direct your thoughts towards the direction you would like to go, you will be able to create anything you wish to in your life. I became fascinated by this law. I began researching a lot of celebrities and discovered an abundance of stories and actors discussing the same idea. Whatever you are focusing on for a long time, you will be able to experience it. There is a tiny percentage of people in the world who achieve the top position and get rewarded unlike other. They have mastered these guidelines and followed them each day. They considered it to be as important as washing your teeth or taking shower.

I researched Will Smith, Arnold Schwarzenegger, Jim Carey, Oprah Winfrey and LMFAO and they all knew about the secret law. They imagined what they would like to have every day, and that's the reason they live the life of their goals. If you'd like to live the life you want, you must act as if you've already got it right now. You must take whatever steps necessary to alter your attitude towards the cost of money from 'I'm unable to afford it' to'money just flows in my direction, I am wealthy. Making small daily changes to your language will improve your outcomes.

Jim Carey was a professional comedian for over a decade, but he struggled to make ends meet and was in debt. There were so many people around him who told that he would succeed and accomplish so many things in his lifetime. He would imagine each night of everything he desired to achieve in his life. He would think about it as if it had already occurred. In the end, he made himself a cheque of $10,000,000 and put it in a date for thanks for 1995. This was three years away. He performed this visualization each day, and in 1995 it was discovered that the amount he would earn $10,000,000 off dumb and more dumb.

These stories are inspirational and can alter your perspective to what is feasible in the world. Write down everything you would like to see in your life and take a trip within your head to think about what you'd like to achieve with no limitations. When I do this , I set aside an hour to just write about the life I'd like to live. What I would like to experience and how much money I can earn and then I write all this in great detail.

Once you've finished the exercise, you can close your eyes and imagine what your goal might be like as well as sound and feel like. Then, just experience the feeling of the end product. I use this three times per each day for my goals, and I have seen the results of all the things I've concentrated on up to this point. I never would have believed that six months ago that I would have achieved the present situation which is why I am extremely passionate about this topic and am encouraging everyone else to try this as often as is possible.

The more time you have to find the time to complete these exercises and the more convinced you are of that. I'd like you to obsess over your goals keep your eyes on it day in and day out and feel as if you have it. If you are able to reach that point, then resources, people and opportunities will begin popping into your mind.

One way to understand the law of attraction is to take a look at Aladdin and his Lamp and then when Aladdin touches the lamp,, a Genie appears. The same happens to us when we shut our eyes and imagine the things we would like to achieve. If we make a wish, that the Universe or Genie appears and does its best to bring our desires to life. It's just like the moment that Aladdin states the wish he would like to see happen, and the Genie responds straight away, 'your wishes are my command and will bring about precisely what he wants.

The first step to the law of attraction is to ASK to be asked what it is you want , so that your brain and universe can have an idea of what they want to attract. Then , you must answer the second one which is that you have to believe that it's possible to manifest. Through changing your thinking and imagining what you want every day, your perception of the possibilities is going to change.

The third step in the law of attraction is to Receive what you're seeking. Every day, you should begin to thank the universe for creating your dream life. Make this a habit and you will feel the abundance of life you are creating.

Law of Attraction 3 Keys
1. Ask
2. Believe
3. Receive

Chapter 7: The Way Our Brains Function

We all think constantly and the thoughts and thoughts that flood the mind of a person directly impact their actions and consequently their situation in life.
When individuals are asked to visualize their thoughts, they tend to imagine the image that follows ... A brain.

The brain is an organ within the body, and it does certain relaying tasks to ensure that the body is functioning correctly. It's certainly an element of our mind the body, spirit, consciousness, but not our brain. Its brain Albert Einstein was examined and it appeared to be just like all other brains.

The inner workings of the mind remain a mystery to the majority of people. The majority of people are in the state of confusion.
Because!

"Mind" is an activity That's Not a It's a.

In the following pages, I'll show you what I've learned about the way your brain works. I'll also show how you can make use of the new information to alter the outcomes you're getting from your daily life.

Meet the "Stick Man." "...

Many people are surprised the "Stick man" offers them a picture to work with in order to comprehend the inner workings of their minds.

"Stick Man" was an idea that was developed in the mind of the Dr. Thurman Fleet, of Santonio Texas in 1934. It was Dr. Fleet was the founder of a personal development method known as "Concept Therapy". "The" Stick Man has also been employed in the past by Bob Proctor and several others.

As you will see, the mind has two distinct parts.
It is the Conscious Mind (CM) and
It is the Sub-Conscious Mind (SM)

Your Conscious Mind

The part in your brain that thinks and reason. It is the sole thing that differentiates "human" consciousness from other animals in the world.

You are able of being able to "choose" your thoughts, you are free to choose your own and the power to think and create.

Your outcomes in life depend on your choices of thoughts however, your thinking is completely influenced by the contents of your subconscious mind.

What you think your identity as a person is actually reflective of the inner content of your subconscious mind.

The brains of children operate differently and they don't have conscious thoughts (beta neural waves) until around seven years of age. This is an important stage in the development of the person we're today.

I'll give you a quick explanation.

Your Sub-Conscious Mind

The sub-conscious mind refers the various mental processes or processes taking place which we aren't conscious of taking place. It is the place where our habits are. This is where we save the routine actions and reactions, such as smoking a smoking cigarette or driving with no thought.

The sub-conscious mind of your brain is an enormous recording device which captures everything you experience, see as well as smell, hear smell and feel. There is also an additional sense that you may have felt.

In reality, the subconscious mind can detect, file and store 100 million bits of information every second!

Imagine it this way:

If you took an excursion through the most crowded portion of the central area of a city such as Paris or Chicago during lunchtime on a weekday it would take a picture of all the shops, the contents of the shops, the cars, their colors and model, and each person who was there, their clothes as well as the expressions they had that they displayed on their faces.

It keeps all of it, including your thoughts, feelings, and even your emotions!

As adults, we've created mental filters. We only pay attention to the things we choose to concentrate on, however, your subconscious mind is able to see every single thing! !

It's a fact that every single person is equipped with an extremely powerful computing device ever existed between our ears. In fact, it is believed by some researchers that even the most smart users don't use even the power of 5. Here's the computer's fate...

It is wrongly programmed!

This is the way it works ....

To understand the way this takes place, it is necessary to look at the development of the mind from the age of three to.

As soon as a child is born the child is born with a consciousness and it has an unconscious mind. The unconscious mind is devoid.

Many people believe that children begin to learn the moment it is born, however some believe that children begin to learn during the womb.

No matter how you think about it, the speed of learning will begin after it is created and is fully to the world of physical reality.

As adults, starts to acquire information through every sense. i.e. Hearing, sight of taste, touch, and, I believe, the sixth sense. This is the time to begin to form your own self-concept.

Two drawings will provide you with an idea of what's going on.

We've all heard that the mind of a child is capable of being influenced, but what is the threshold of being influenced?

When a baby is born, it is the Pure as well as a Clean Mind ....It's like the blank paper.
If you're young when you are young, your family members like parents or aunts and uncles as well as siblings and brothers will give you specific instructions. The instructions are similar to these:

"Don't Do this" (or "don't do this" or "don't do that" as well as "No! You shouldn't do that" or

"No you can't do this".

The word parents use the most often is "No".

"Researchers believe that the average child receives around twenty negative comments from parents for each positive, reassuring, and reassuring one."

Then, they speak about you, right in your face as if you were not there and make statements like:

"He's a bad kid"
"He does not get along with other kids"
"He's so painful and he's always crying"
"She's such a loud child, she won't stop talking".

As you grow older, you hear things like:

"She isn't very coordinated. She'll never become an expert dancer" or
"He's in a state of despair with maths He'll likely fail the next time" or
"You're not competent enough to run your own business. Do an excellent job and let the business take care of you."

This type of negative programming got directly to your unconscious mind...

They swung straight into the highly impressionable subconscious mind.
We generally don't know what program occurred.
We know that children will not be aware of it and accept it as factual.

Of course, they've spoke of positive things... however, it's not enough.

Everything you feel or heard is kept in the memory of your unconscious mind. I'm talking about everything.

It keeps track of all the radio, television as well as the books, comics, and any other information that you come in contact with.

It documents the words your siblings, brothers aunties, uncles, teachers, and other friends said.

However, the most important thing is...

Take special note of the things I'm going to speak next...

The subconscious mind stores and highlights all data "The The Child" receives that has an emotional aspect to it, for example,

"You must work hard for it"
"Hard work is reward"
"Money isn't a tree"
"You must work hard to earn the money"
"We're poor, but we're happy"
"I am miserable at the job I do, however, I've no other choice"
"We must stay with the sake of our children"
"Everyone with money has to have deceived someone"
"Only the most evil of people can afford to buy"
"Rich people are those who have taken advantage of everyone"
"You must be in early and be home by late before you can go in late and leave early"

The term "e-motion" is an abbreviation to mean energy that moves. although a child might not understand the meaning of the meanings or words, it is able to sense the emotion and energy of the words being spoken.

The whole process takes place from the time you are born until age seven. It is also known as"the "Imprint Ages" and around the age of seven at the age of seven, it is when the "conscious" mind starts to form. This is when researchers believe that the mind begins to make beta waves, and begins making decisions or making judgments regarding whether something is true or not.

The information, thoughts and emotions we are exposed to during those "imprint years" are bound to a state and are out of our minds. The term "state bound" means that, for memories to return to our consciousness it is necessary to be in the same state of mind that we were in at the time it happened. Therefore, it remains in our main file of thoughts, feelings as well as sounds and sights, but we do not know that it exists. This master file is utilized by our computer brain to determine the meaning of the events, and to make decisions regarding their significance. Our response to the happenings in our lives determines the way you live your life. This can be said to be subconscious or unconscious.

The new programming, good or not, will continue to run throughout your life, however the basic principles are established in the first 21 years. The old programming will guide you until you take a the decision to alter it. Find out the best way to alter it and, most importantly, Make the effort to change your thoughts or your old programming!!!

In the first 21 years of your life your life is a series of emotions, conditioned responses behavior, attitudes and values. It is the point at which you develop your own beliefs, who you are as well as your values, persona, or who you are.

The elephant is a great example of negative imprinting training. Let's take a look at the process. Have you been to a circus and witnessed a massive elephant guided by a small chain that was attached to a tiny stake that is buried on the ground? It's evident that the elephant could simply move the stake to be free!

But, the elephant can't perform this, since when he was just a baby and the trainer put an enormous chain around his leg with the big stake into the earth. No matter how hard the elephant pulled, it could not free himself. This taught the elephant that it was pointless to try to gain free. The idea becomes so powerful in the mind of the animal ... it is the reason they've been known to die in a campfire due to the belief that it is ineffective to pull that stake.

"We all live in a box made of our own creation
The issue is the instructions for getting out of the box.
Prints are on the outside of the box."
(Unknown)

Much like the elephant, it's not the actual events of our lives that define our lives, but the beliefs we hold regarding what these events have to do with. This makes the entire process more complex and, as a result, it's difficult to comprehend. Each person creates the box of their choice.

In his book "Awaken the Giant Within" Tony Robins relates this story "He was cruel and bitter, an alcoholic and a drug addict who was close to committing suicide many times. He is currently serving the life sentence in prison to be convicted of the killing of a cashier in a liquor store who "got stuck in the middle". Two sons are his, born just eleven months apart. One of whom went on to become "just the same as Dad" addicted to drugs who hid his wealth and terrorizing others until he as well, was thrown in prison as a result of an attempted murder.

However, his brother is quite the opposite man who is raising three children and is enjoying his marriage and seems to be genuinely content. As a regional director for an important national company He finds his job equally challenging and satisfying. He is physically fit and does not have any substance or alcohol addictions!

What could these two men of the same age have turned out in such a different way after having been raised in the same place online? Both were asked in private without knowing each other. "Why have your lives turned into this way?" Surprisingly, they each gave the exact response: "What else could I be if I had been raised with such a father?"

We are often lulled to believe that circumstances determine our lives, and our environment is the one that has made us our present. A few people believe that it's the fault of their parents for their inability to live the life they want to live. There is no greater lie that has ever been said! It's not what happens in our lives that define us, but rather our perceptions about what these events are about.

I had a fascinating experience several years in the past. It was the case that a few from my brothers and me got together just a few days before the reunion of the family. We hired a van and went on a trip to our town of birth as well as the place

that we were raised in. The most remarkable thing was that every person had a different perception of the events that occurred while we grew older. At times, I believed that we shouldn't be talking about the exact same experiences.
The impression we left on our minds were the thoughts we felt about the incident and, often, how our emotions varied greatly regarding the identical incident. The children who were younger may have felt fearful but the more experienced had completely different feelings about the same event.
It was not the actual events in our life that imprinted on us, but our beliefs regarding what these events implied. It was incredible!
"Change begins with a decision to implement the changes." Anthony Robbins

Chapter 8: What Are The Benefits Of Lucid Dreaming?

Archimedes, the man who was credited with figuring out the method of solving problems, without contemplating them actually fell asleep in the bath that clarified his thoughts it is a mystery to time. But, just lying down and relaxing, or meditating, or taking a stroll and not thinking about "the issue" to be solved is an ancient method of using to solve issues. Scientists, writers, and engineers frequently claim that the spark they required came by simply stopping searching for it. A lot of people, particularly those working in the creative industry are likely to keep the notebook next to their bed in order to record any interesting ideas. The majority of writers will confess to keeping notebooks at all times because inspiration and thoughts are always at hand but it's usually not a practical one!

Creativity in Problem-Solving, and Lucid Dreaming
For the majority of people who have had at least one occasion during their lifetime, the sensation of waking up and finding an answer to an issue that has been bothering them for a long time is an experience that is familiar to all. This is, in a

way, the reason our unconscious mind appears to be designed for. If you're faced with a challenge in your life (big as or minor) the more you concentrate on it while awake, the more serious it becomes. The solution is also becoming more difficult to find, and even more. If you do, however, go to sleep contemplating the issue and it's likely that at night, you'll discover the answer to you. You might not even be having a dream about the problem (though it's likely that you did) however, when you wake up your brain has sorted through the issue in a more calm, sensible way, and has found the answer.

It is thought that Lucid Dreaming can allow you to access this problem-solving aspect of your mind more effectively and directly. It is also believed that during our subconscious time, we're more adept in coming up with creative solutions for any problem. Studies on the phenomenon are currently scarce and infrequent, however, some studies have shown (Burke and Shaw[1(1)] the fact that Lucid Dreamers demonstrate around 25 percent improvement in solving problems. Although the capability to tackle problems as you sleep is attainable for anyone (it is in fact, what we humans do) getting access to the imaginative, intuitive and imaginative part of our minds and conscious of its functioning when we sleep provides us with the opportunity to control our subconscious mind to perform the task that we want to accomplish. While it is not just enhancing our ability to solve problems This benefit of Lucid Dreaming can assist us to solve specific problems quickly and assist us in becoming just more effective throughout our lives.

Stress Relief

The time of dreams is when we reflect on all the happenings that happen in our lives and are a time that we're most at peace. When it comes to easing stress, the verdict isn't yet in however it is likely you'll find that Lucid Dreaming may be an effective method to manage the stresses and strains of everyday life. It's also been suggested that acquiring the methods of Lucid Dreaming could aid you in dealing with more complex stress-related problems and issues. In a nutshell If you are able to manage your dreams and manage stress, you can beat it by creating a dream vacation for yourself. There's no usual limitations to consider when choosing your destination. Hawaii, Havana or another world are all within reach once the ability to are able to master Lucid

Dreaming. There's no hassle with baggage and travel can be done in a flash! In times of stress in your life, you can arrange an excursion to a place you believe will lessen stress. You'll get there in only minutes!

On a more serious level, the use of Lucid Dreaming as a technique for combating conditions such as Post-Traumatic-Stress-Disorder (PTSD) has recently been explored. Numerous studies were conducted in recent years and all are concluding the following: Lucid Dreaming techniques are an effective way to combat nightmares. While several research studies (Spoormaker as well as van den Bout[22] have confirmed this, it's unclear how this technique works. It does appear that the ability to reduce anxiety in dreams is a highly positive side effect of Lucid Dreaming. Nightmare Control
Related to this control of our dreams naturally allows us to "stop" nightmares from happening. The effects of nightmares are universal, sometimes they are caused by your fears (real as well as imagined) manifesting. Our brains try to inform us "what's the most frightening thing that could occur" or to express these fears in the

secure space of sleeping. But for those who have suffered for years of nightmares it is far from relaxing. Controlling your thoughts through conscious involvement in them could provide important relief from the nighttime horror films. It doesn't mean that you are absconding, or avoiding the issue, but rather storing the issue to deal with it the future. Once you've mastered the issue, you'll be able tackle the problem that's causing the problem in a more productive, safe, and imaginative method.

Physical Skills

Training or learning new physical abilities is exhausting. However when we're sleeping, we're at peace. In a study by Danial Erlacher and Michael Schredl[3], it was discovered that Lucid Dreamers competent enough to perform a basic task while they were dreaming could enhance their abilities in the real world. The task was to throw coins in a glass. participants were required be able to finish the task before going to sleep. Lucid Dreamers were asked to keep practicing throughout their sleep. They were later tested on their accuracy after awakening. The Lucid Dreamer group showed a significant improvement in their skill over earlier in the day. Tossing coins into cups is not a huge task. But there are numerous Lucid Dream proponents argue that it is possible to practice any kind of sport, job, or exercise in the sleep when you've developed the ability to control your dreams. In actuality, this makes sense on a number of levels. The neural pathways are formed during the practice of any skill, and as according to psychologists that our brains aren't able to distinguish the difference between "real" as opposed to "unreal"activity. While some might think that this is tiring Lucid Dreamers report that whatever their active and clear dreams may be, they feel more energized than ever before once they've learned the art.

Fear and Phobias

The majority of fears and phobias you experience in your life aren't as genuine as they appear. Fear is a normal human reaction and an extremely useful one. However, it could become uncontrollable and, when it does the fear transforms into anxiety. Lucid Dreaming can be utilized to overcome our fears and confront these fears. If you're scared of heights, you can imagine leaping off a cliff that is too high cliff or an aircraft. Are you scared? It could be, but in the dream world, where you have control and it is a safe controlled, safe act. You can glide, float or glide towards the floor at your pace. Lucid Dreamers claim that by confronting, taking control and acting out their fears, they notice that their fears in reality are less threatening. It is also likely to be due to the brain creating new neural pathways, allowing us to experience the fear-inducing experience positively and altering our daily reaction.

Conversations with the Dead

The loss of a loved one could be among the most painful experiences anyone goes through throughout our lives. It is a difficult time for anyone. Dreaming is one method that can aid in easing the grief that comes with time. For those who believe in the practice, it is generally believed that connecting with lost loved ones we dream about can help us to heal both on a psychological and emotional level. If you acknowledge that it's your mental state that is "creating" the experience it can provide you with time and space to speak the words you have to say and slowly release the person who is in question. Lucid Dreaming is a method to cope with grief can be particularly helpful in cases where the loss was sudden or unexpected . It provides us with the opportunity to confront the loss in a creative, productive and positive way to achieve a sense of closure. This is due partly due to the way our brains process dreams. they are less able to distinguish in between "real" and "not real" and perceive both kinds of consciousness as separate aspects of the same experience of reality. In the moment of consciousness, you might recognize the encounter you had with a loved one was a dream but deep in your brain, the memory will be a constant and become real. It is fascinating to know that many people be experiencing this kind of Lucid Dream in what may be described as the term "waking nightmare". In the aftermath of a sudden loss, it is common for people to "see" and communicate with your loved one who has passed away. Psychologists are not shy about accepting this reality and simply see it as a way to assist us in our grief process. Making use of this technique in the form of Lucid Dreaming could be extremely useful indeed.

Creative Expressions

Human beings are naturally creative We wouldn't have gotten up to the point we're at today without our creativity. But, not all of us are as well-informed the creative aspect of our personalities as other people. In fact, it is believed that a lot of our creativity abilities are controlled by the subconscious, which is the creative part of our brain. When we practice Lucid Dreaming techniques we are connected to the brain's creative side and can access it whenever we want. The free flow of thoughts that flow from this region of the brain can be stimulating and also extremely educational. Lucid Dreamers usually have a shift in direction in their lives, and discover that they possess hidden talents and abilities that they never thought of. Every aspect of life that needs creativity (and many have) can be improved by Lucid Dreaming techniques.

Chapter 9: Illustrations To Prosperity, Wealth And The Pursuit Of Success

The Cave of Money
You're walking through the forest beneath a lush canopy of green trees. The sun shines through the foliage as you can feel the warmth of it warming. You continue walking until you spot the cave, which has a massive wooden door. You grab its intricate metal handle, and then begin to turn it , and the door opens independently. When you reach the threshold, a sense of peace is felt over you. Within this cave you can see that the wooden door is open. Just a few steps further you are greeted by a warm sensation and then you see an enthralling white light that is coming out of the ceiling. A throne-like chair is fixed to the ground, in the middle of the light beams that emanate through the ceiling.

You sit comfortably on the cushion of burgundy and lay your hands on the gold armrests. You suddenly utter your wish for prosperity, wealth and a life that is free from routine work to afford the necessities.

A scene that resembles film screens before you: rooms of cash packed into massive, unreal piles that seem to continue for ever. You reach out and rub the ridges of bills that are closest to you. The scent of money is in your airways. Paper stacks that are soft green with ridges to the extent they can be seen. You grab the stack and look through the cash in your pocket. What do you think you can do with it? Feel free, happy leaving your job and assist people within your family, yourself or someone else on the street? There are so many amazing possibilities. The bills are ablaze before your eyes with no outstanding balances, or "paid in complete" written on them. What a wonderful feeling!

It's raining money
While walking down the street you open your umbrella and your shirt gets flecked with drops of rain. You cautiously steer clear of a massive splashes of water from earlier rain, as you get from the curb to traverse the street. Then you head to the bank hoping that they'll give you a credit line so that you can purchase the item you've always wanted. A $10 bill lies on the ground before you. If you look around, but you don't see anyone who could have dropped it. You stoop down to grab it and put it into your pocket. The rain is more intense now and you are giddy for having thought of bringing some protection

against it. You observe a man on the street getting wet. You hear an "thud" as something crashes into your umbrella and close to knocking it off your hand. Your eyes are closed and you return them to verify the image you have spotted the same thing: a $1 dollars, almost directly in front of you. This time , you're excited but are hesitant to grab it. You gaze across the street hoping that someone will come running toward you. The scene you see is difficult to understand as people are kneeling into the ground or speeding to collect large amounts of money. Some are standing around staring at the sky. Raining cash is actually happening. It's a good thing there aren't a lot of people around, as it continues to pour and pour rain. You attempt to stay at peace and begin to collect loose bills and wads as you walk down the street, not worried about securing a money at the banks. You open your back pack and begin to stuff money into it, without noticing that your bills are damp.

The Trees that produce money are the ones that grow.
There's a small tree you've planted in your garden or yard. Maybe it's in a container inside your home, where there's space. It could be any kind

of tree you'd love. You take care of it as any other tree-loving enthusiast ensure that it has enough soil, water, sunlight and nutrients. The tree will grow and, in time, it becomes rich and beautiful with beautiful green leaves. One day, you spot the remains of a dollar note next to the trunk's bottom. You grab it without remembering that you dropped any cash. When you next walk through, you see additional money at the bottom of the tree. You glance up and realize that there aren't only leaves, but money sprouting from the branches. You climb an incline and begin picking the cash that is waiting as if it were fruit.

Smart Money
You let your money work for you, and you use your money wisely. Every time you get paid, there is the option of putting a portion to a savings account or another account that you don't be able to access but you can keep track of it to see the amount increase (and perhaps earn some interest). You may indulge in treats from time to time however, you shouldn't spend your money on things that you don't really need. When you visit the shop, you can find sales and usually get the items you require at a reasonable cost. You may even be able to use coupons. You can stock

up when you spot a deal on items are used often. You can save money on fuel by combining trips and you rarely need to visit the market to purchase just a few items. Bring your lunch or food with you to work, so you don't have to eat at restaurants all the time. You may listen to your family members, friends or coworkers complain they're broke or have spent all of their money. This can make you feel down, but you are also happy at yourself for not having been in the same situation, even although you're not proud of it. If someone asks how you are able to not break even You are able to share the secret.

You get more enthusiastic about saving money rather than spending it. You seem to be able to come up with new strategies to reduce your expenses. You're smart about your money.

Time to Save

You've had a good day. Everything seemed flowing. The day is coming to an end. You've just finished your satisfying dinner and are getting ready for the next day. You've got your clothes prepared, along with any other items you'll need. Now, flash forward to when you rise and start preparing for the next day and then get to where you're headed. You've had a great night's sleep.

You wake fresh and energetic and looking forward to what the day may bring. You start getting ready and everything you require is available, because of the earlier preparation. When you get to work, to an appointment or where you need to go you look up the time and notice that you're ahead of the schedule. You are proud of yourself to be punctual while not needing to hurry. You can go through every stoplight on your way to your destination and still arrive on time with plenty of time left.

Difficult Person Neutralizer
There are always the grumpy guy or gal at work, or perhaps a place we are required to visit regularly. Perhaps it's someone from your family. It could be that she is a complete woman pet (sorry canines) or he could be the most pompous of a sexy guy or a sexy jerk, but whatever this person is, it's difficult to be around them for long. It might be a bit obnoxious but you're not sending the person any harm or harm in this situation. You're simply neutralizing the current influence they exert on you, and having a blast by doing so. What's the point of giving your power to them and allow yourself to become depressed or unhappy? You may find that this or similar

imagery can reduce or eliminate the anxiety that you feel every time you meet the person.

Here's the deal. You are free to make this as outrageous as you want, and actually it's advised, just make sure you don't cause anyone any harm. This lets you attack any power they may have over you (figuratively obviously) and therefore reducing its grip on you.

Let's assume that your boss is. To simplify this exercise, let's say it's a man. Imagine him wearing ridiculous clothes such as Teenage Mutant Ninja Turtles or Hello Kitty. What about coffee and mustard stains all over his clothes? What would you think the person who suddenly stopped being able for making you feel awful or stressed, or whatever they make you feel? It's like a super-hero who has had the power of a super hero taken away. Imagine a person leaving the bathroom with toilet paper sticking to his shoes as well as long pieces of trailing paper with some mysterious stains. Ewww! What about every machine is touched by him malfunctions, such as the copier, the computer, or even the phone? You'll get the idea. Keep it funny, silly and safe.

Visualizations for health

Mother earth
While sitting on the dirt or grass and you can feel your body's connection to the earth. The sun warms your body and the breeze touches your face. The roots start to sprout at the base of your spine, and work their way through the soil. A feeling of connection and belonging is felt over you. You feel at peace and realize that you are a part of and purpose in the world. All your worries and worries are released from your roots and into earth. The earth's emits love and a feeling of belonging. This feeling is transmitted through the roots until the feeling is able to reach your heart. The roots are drawn back until they are buried in the bottom of your spine. You feel complete and have you feel a profound sense of gratitude. You are complete and perfect.

Light laser
As you lie at ease on a bed or gurney, each piece of your body feels completely relaxed. You are confident that you're at the right spot and are at

home here. Warmth blankets your body at the perfect temperature. You look up for a moment and you can see a shining light stream over you. You notice that regardless of the area of the body you are thinking about, light is moving around it. Like many may be, you've got a few minor, or even serious health concerns you want to tackle. Choose one of the areas and the light will follow towards the area of your body. It moves around the region with laser accuracy and then moves toward the center until it's touched each and every cell of the area. Then, in your mind's eye, you are able to see the problem slowly dissolving, becoming shrinking and less. You decide to repeat the process which is very enjoyable.

Every time you perform this practice, the issue is in your mind's eye, regardless of whether you discern it or not appears to dissolve.

You ask yourself why you didn't realized this sooner However, it doesn't bother you. You're grateful for any relief or resolution that you get.

Human Sun

When you are lying in a comfortable mattress or on a gurney a warm lamp sits just only a few feet over you. in perfect alignment, radiating warming warmth to your whole body. Your body is wrapped in soft, sheets that are clean. Your body is relaxed and comfortable. Every time you inhale the light gradually fills your body, till your entire body filled with light and pleasant warmth. After each exhalation, all troubles, disharmonies or unhappiness go away until your body is perfectly balanced and is filled with sparkling white light.

Lightening Body
You're standing in a fieldwith your feet are bare to the ground. The sky is dark and one huge grey cloud is positioned just above your head. A flash of lightning erupts from it, and illuminates the sky briefly before another. The third flash gently and harmlessly comes into contact with to the crown of your head, and brightens every cell in your body. You feel alive and euphoric. After a short time smoke rises from your head, as negative energy and all disorder or discord leaves your body and your spirit. Your whole being is cleansed and renewed on every level.

Lose weight
There are many who are in need of food all over the world However, removing food from your plate isn't going assist them even a bit. If you keep doing it regularly enough, it could harm you

in the end You know this, at on some level.
It's a familiar feeling when you're stressed, you go to the store for something for a snack, in order to alleviate the pressure. You go for cookies or potato chips, candy as well as a sandwich with ham, or any of the countless other items you could be able to grab in the vicinity for snacking. There's something relaxing and comfortable about food. Your clothes might be getting smaller and you might not be pleased with your body however when you're feeling stressed, you need relief in the form of something tasty to eat.

It's a grand buffet that has every type of food that you could imagine. You stroll around the tables and marvel at every dish. You set some spoons of all the food that interests the taste buds of your. In your dining room there is only a small amount remaining on the plate you have a couple of bites, taking in and enjoying each bite. Soon, you realize that you're beginning to feel full. After a few more bites, you are ready to leave, with your plate partially covered. You are satisfied, but maybe feeling a bit guilty for not putting food items on your table but it's fine. You imagine to yourself that maybe you'll be used to this amazing feeling of being satisfied and full, but not overly full.

Healthy Shopping

You walk into a store and then take the cart. You load your cart with fresh fruits and vegetables as well as other healthy food items. You walk through aisles filled with junk food without making a stop. You've been doing this without buying any unhealthy food items when you shop for groceries for a few weeks and now. You notice that you're feeling more relaxed and your clothes seem a bit looser. You are happy with how you appear and feel, and it's normal to buy your groceries this way as it doesn't require any effort to avoid the temptations of food that used to tempt you. There's no need to be tempted by a indulgence, but it won't make you go over the edge into craving more. You're happy with what's in your grocery cart and what you're feeding your body.

Healthy Cooking

In your kitchen , or in your friend's kitchen or in the kitchen of a friend, you are about cook your food item. It can be whatever the stomach (and stomach) would like. Even the food that is not cooked and prepared the food you are eating is stunning. There are cut pieces of meat which are hormone-free fresh, chemical free, and chemical free. If you're a vegetarian, you can enjoy delicious beans, legumes , and nuts. The aromas of different spices fill your nostrils when you decide which one to choose. When you look to one side of the room and see an array of brightly colored vegetables, including green leafy leaves and yellow, red and orange vegetables. They're a literal rainbow of hues. You and anyone you're with chop, cut and lay out the food before putting them in your oven. When it's all done and set sitting on the table, you can smell the aroma of every dish. Everyone is amazed at the deliciousness of everything as they eat their meals. While you're eating, you take in every bite, chewing deeply before swallowing it, taking in its delicious, nutritious warm sensation as it flows through your mouth. It's so delicious that you want to take it in and not be rushed. Then you'll feel satisfied and content, but not overly full.

Chapter 10: Control Your Emotions To Be Happier

By your emotions you are in control of your emotional vibration. If you alter your frequency, it alters your perception. This means that what that you see and the way in which you view things shifts.

What does your world look like when you're depressed? And what happens when you're happy and in good spirits? If you're depressed, everything around you looks bleak and things don't go as planned. If you're happy the world appears bright and things go according to plan. The fundamentals: Your thoughts turn into images. Actually, we think in images and trigger emotions. Your emotions are the reason for the frequency of your emotional vibration. Your vibration frequency is the reason for the perception you get.

These are the key components that control your life. These elements are called variables. They are able to fluctuate. The variables that are all interconnected. That means that if one variable is changed, all other variables also change. The variables emotion and frequency of vibration are linked by a coefficient of 100 percent. This means that the more you boost your emotional state, so how much your frequency increases.

The thought (picture) is emotion is the frequency of vibration is the way in which one perceives oneself and the world around him.

A thought could be neutral, positive, or negative. It could cause you to feel worse or better. It can lift you up, and trigger another kind of emotion within you.

The frequency of your emotional vibration changes depending on how you feel. It could be high, low or anything in between, increasing or decreasing.

Positive thoughts create positive emotions and the associated frequency of vibrations. This can change your perception and it will show to your mind as positive transformation of your life. Check in with yourself: If you are thinking negative thoughts What made you feel before? What are your thoughts when you're not feeling good? When you have about negative things, then you be less content. The shift in the way you feel could be small however it could trigger an unending cycle. If you are feeling less than good and you feel negative, you begin to think about it. The cycle goes on. When you think an optimistic thought What did you think of feeling shorter prior to this? What do you think of when you feel great? If you focus on positive thoughts, you'll feel great. Anything you choose to do it will get better. It makes you feel more relaxed. If you are feeling good it is easier to are more positive and positive. Positive circles are activated.

Your thoughts are influenced by not just by your thoughts and thoughts, but also by everything that you experience, witness and smell from the your surroundings, as well as the areas and locations where you live or pass through.

Pay attention to the information that comes into your body, as it can affect your life and the way you live it.
1. What you can see, hear or taste.
2. What people are around you?
3. Locations where you can visit or pass through
4. Your shoes and clothes
5. The fabric of your carpet and furniture
6. What do you do

Imagine that everything has an electromagnetic radiation that can affect your emotional the vibration.

If you have a TV or radio running it will feed everything you can hear and see into your computer. Similar to the internet. If you don't listen attentively, it will operate in a subliminal way. Have you ever wondered what caused your mood to disappeared suddenly? Perhaps you wondered what you paid for that type of food item, like sweets, that were not on your list of items to buy?

Avoid watching or listening to anything that can cause negative emotions. This includes news stories about atrocities, and films about crime and horror. There's so much available on television and on the internet that you could pick the content that inspires positive emotions. When you see the news on television there are situations that aren't good for your health. It is more easy to accept the negative side of living a healthier way of life. It is therefore not surprising that people want to hear negative news. If you're not experiencing a major disaster It seems to you that you're in good shape and the shock factor of news that is bad be interesting. How often do you notice something positive happening in the news? What would you think of your reaction when the news only convey positive news, such as an example, a stunning wedding or an upcoming birth, new baby in town, the weather in the last year was great for wine, information about the latest innovations, new books and more? Do you view your news channel with as much excitement as you would the normal negative news? Do you think: "Why should I be concerned, even if last year's weather was great for wine? If I'm looking to purchase an ebook, I check the latest books released." I can hear you! But how do you know that a thousand miles away was a crash which involved twenty vehicles? Don't get me wrong. You must be educated. Find how different it is to watch horrific situations and becoming aware. Don't watch the entire news on television. There is no way to help anyone in the event that your mood is deteriorating. You can assist, if you feel good in your emotional well-being and vibration increases, and when you're energetic and have brilliant ideas to generate more income. You must, of course, be aware. Check the internet for a newspaper , look over the headlines, and if it is necessary or you would like to learn more about the article.

Be aware of the people you live in and whom you get to meet. Make sure you choose your friends wisely. If you know a person who is frequently down and who often complains and constantly harping about issues, don't talk to him. There is an unfavorable vibration that emits and can have a negative effect on your. This is a crucial question is: Are you a positive person ? And do you radiate positive energy?

Make a wise choice about the places you visit. If you are not a fan of an establishment, bar, or cafe, go elsewhere and search for a place that makes you are comfortable. If you are unhappy with something in the shopping mall or retail store, walk away and move on to another.

Every thing has its own unique frequency of vibration. It is the same for every thought all objects, every shade, and even every single piece of our being. The most important factor in the way you see things and how you live your life and the things you own, how you earn money, and all other aspects of your life is your frequency of vibration in your mind. When I refer to that frequency in the class I'm referring to the frequency of vibration that affects your emotions. The frequency of your vibration changes in the course of a day and throughout the entire year, but it remains within a specific bandwidth. If you improve your mental health and remain there for a couple of months or even weeks in a row, your vibration frequency will increase. Due to your increased frequency of vibration your life and you will be transformed positively.

A person who leads a particular lifestyle has a particular frequency. If you'd like to live according to a particular way of life you must adapt the frequency you use according to your particular lifestyle. How? Find the joy of the lifestyle you would like to live , and your well-being and happiness should be in harmony with the way of living the lifestyle you wish to lead.

In order to change your life for your advantage, you must to be in control of your thoughts all that is a part of your body and discover ways to increase the level of vibrance. The higher your frequency, the more vibration which increases your well-being and happiness. The circle is now closed. You are in charge of your health and your happiness by your thoughts, the things you do, and everything that surrounds you, and radiates towards you.

You can't change an increase in frequency to go from a low frequency to a more high one overnight. Improve your health and happiness to a certain extent and then become accustomed to the sensation, and then proceed to raise them again gradually and become accustomed to the feeling that is now an entirely new level of status. Each step will make you feel lighter, like you were carrying heavy baggage on your back. It is becoming lighter.If you can feel more content and remain in a more positive frame of mind, anything you set out to accomplish can be accomplished faster and with less effort. If you attempt to do something when you're not feeling well, it's as being as if you've put only one hand on the accelerator, and the other one on the brake.

If you increase your well-being level and happiness over time, you'll be surprised by how you feel and how much more easy to achieve everything you want. accomplished.

Every day, there are hard and challenging times. These moments won't be absent from your life however they won't cause you to feel so down like previously. Your frequency of vibration in your emotions is not going to go too low and won't remain low for long.

What's your current mood? What would you like to feel?
Have you ever been incredibly content? Imagine you feel exactly like that, and perhaps even happier.

If you can control your thoughts, you are in control of your emotions.
Your emotions shouldn't drop to levels that are too low. Do not dwell on negative feelings for long. If you don't feel at ease, do something that will make you feel happier and concentrate your thoughts to something positive.

Be happy forever!
Don't put any restrictions on your happiness. Don't claim that you'd be more content in the event of something particular happening. Do your best to be happy without a reason . Make it a routine to be and stay satisfied. Be aware of everything that is amazing. Consider yourself in a position where you're at the top of your success and happiness future. You will feel a pleasant anticipation.
Take a break from reading and reflect on what makes you feel happy and what makes you feel happy in your ideal life.

Create a list of everything that feels good about writing. Then, divide this list into
• What is the best way to ensure you feel well during your work time?
• What can you do to make yourself feel at ease when you're far from home?
And what could you be doing to be comfortable when you're home?
If you are feeling that your mood has dropped Do something to get better. If needed, review your Feel-Good-List.
I have mentioned that you must be happy forever and that you must always be content. You can also be more joyful. Feel as content as you can be after the dream you've had will come true.

Find the feeling of what you would like!
What exactly is it that you are being in"the "Feeling of what you'd like"? What is it like to be thin? What is it like to earn a significant amount of money per month? What does it feel like to have a partner who is a true love? What is it like to feel you're extremely successful in your work? How do you feel when you be famous? It's likely that you do not know.
Research and study peoplewho have achieved what you're looking for. If you are looking to shed

weight, observe those who have slim bodies. Check out their clothes as well as their movements, and how people react towards them. Find videos of rich people and then watch their lifestyle , and the way they look to you. Ask yourself how you'd like to feel once you've accomplished your biggest target.

When you're picturing an objective, picture your life following the achievement of the objective. Visualizing a new scenario and the way it feels, can assist you to get familiar with it. The reason why you should be afraid of anythingthat is connected to an objective is likely to disappear as well as the motive behind the system's inability to accomplish it. Additionally, the duration and severity of the discomfort will decrease. If the discomfort is not severe the system does not have a reason to prevent the attainment of this goal.

I will repeat this because it's crucial. If you envision the achievement of a objective, you must go one step further which is imagine the life you will live following the achievement of this objective. This means that you don't imagine the moment when you've accomplished your objective, but rather the way your life has changed following the achievement.

Whatever you desire in life, you must increase your vibration in order to attain it. This means that you need to be positive and increase your well-being and the level of happiness you enjoy.
1. Keep your eyes on the bright side.
2. Raise your wellbeing factor
3. You can increase your level of happiness

How do you manage your feelings so that you feel better and happier , and increase the frequency of your vibration?
1. With your thoughts
2. With conditioned stimuli
3. With meditation
4. Anything that helps you feel better.

Be in control of your emotions by controlling your thoughts
Be aware of your thoughts and take control of your thoughts. Focus on positive, positive thoughts. Consider what you like as well as what you do to make yourself smile. Take a look at pictures that inspire positive emotions in you.
If you are aware of an unfavorable thought, swish it off and imagine something you love. You'll do yourself any favors in the event that you think

about negative thoughts. It causes you to feel depressed and makes your heart sink. Additionally, it is a proven fact that if you think about something negative often enough, it will eventually will happen. Don't think about anything you would not like to see in your life.

Be careful about the content you listen and watch. Find what inspires positive emotions. Select happy and positive people to meet. Find places that make you feel comfortable.
If you're angered, consider the reason you were angry. If it's someone else who has angered you, show respect for the perspective of the person. Find out what the person was trying to say the reason you were furious. You might have did not understand some thing. There are times when people are unhappy and wish to cause a negative impact on someone else and say something that could be hurtful. If this is the situation you should turn around and walk away from the person. Be aware that when you're upset your frequency of vibration decreases and that will not be best for you or your future. It is not a good idea to waste time with the person or thing that or that creates negative emotions in you.

Essential requirements to feel great You must choose organic, non-processed food items. Include exercise in your routine. Get enough sleep. Get every day some time for yourself.
If you don't feel at ease, figure out a method to improve your health. It could be a time away, even in the event that it's only an hour or so to relax. It could be a great meal, taking the walk, taking a relaxing bath with a lovely scent, having a coffee with a friend , or whatever else comes to thoughts.

My suggestion: Create an all-inclusive list of things that make you feel good (Feel-Good-List See above) and then make it into a Word document and then save the file. If you need to, look through the list and take action, that makes you feel good.

Chapter 11: Law Of Attraction 101 What Is It And How It Functions

Many people do not recognize that we hold lots of power. Power that, is harnessed in the right way, will allow us to draw into our lives everything we desire and achieve our dreams. The power we're talking about is the potential to harness The Law of Attraction (LOA) which, if utilized correctly will help you create an enjoyable life for yourself.

Understanding the Law of Attraction
Law of Attraction is an universal law that is based on one simple principle, "the tendency to draw toward ourselves what we are most focused on". In simple terms"the law of attraction" stipulates that "like attracts like".

The law basically means that, regardless of whether we are aware of it or acknowledge that fact, we are accountable to bring all kinds influence into our lives. This includes positive and negative ones. Every single one of the failures, successes and achievements, unforgettable experiences as well as the bleak moments we've had are the result of the law and our capacity to attract various experiences as well as the opportunities that go to them for our personal self.

This is due to the power of our minds to transform the things we are focused on into transform it into reality. If we are thinking about the things that has happened in the past, or worrying about what might happen in the future, we'll only create more negative thoughts about ourselves. If we're positive, hopeful, and happy , even though the world is chaotic around us, we'll eventually get over that stressful time and look forward to joyful days.

This law is the reason certain people are capable of overcoming their challenges and bad days swiftly, while others are stuck in the same rut for lengthy period of period of time. There are many people who have similar characteristics to this. They seem to have everything they need with a positive attitude, always smiling with a positive attitude and have faith that the glass will always be half-full. They draw attention to others because people like to be around their positive energy. Many people see this as luck and positive thinking, it is actually what can help these people attract positive experiences and triumph at the final.

Once you've learned is the law of attraction

actually is let's take a examine how it operates.

How the Law Of Attraction Works

We are energy-based beings. Also everything else around us is energy. The energy particles within our bodies and everything around us oscillate at various levels. That means that our thoughts, attitudes and behaviour are all an energy. When energy is vibrating and attracts every energy particle that is vibrating on the same frequency. This happens because of what you pay attention to and the perspective, belief or belief system you place your attention on determines the things that your attention draws towards you.

If you are thinking of something, you begin to create thoughts that are related to it. The thoughts you create travel across the universe, and draw toward them all other thoughts operating on the same frequency; that's how you draw similar experiences to your own.

If you're feeling happy and feeling good inside, your energy field is aligned with the fields of vibration in the universe. This can bring good positive things into your life. Simply say, when you concentrate on the goals you want to achieve, and focus on them in a way that feels good from the inside, these good feelings will draw your goals closer to you.

But, when you don't focus on what you really desire or concentrate on the right goals but with negative emotions bubbling up within you it is difficult to align your energy field with the higher frequency of the universe, and consequently do not draw your goals towards you.

What exactly does this mean? It is a way to bring the love, money, prosperity and happiness it is essential to be positive and happy within yourself so that you match your vibration with that of the universe and draw everything you want from your own self.

Let's see how you can make use of LOA and the the power of your thoughts to create your ideal life. We will begin by examining the ways to utilize LOA to attract joy and love in your current life.

Chapter 12:10 Fantastic Tips For Greater Concentration And Focus

There are other things that you can do to boost your focus, besides taking part in regular meditation. Here is a list of 10 amazing strategies you can follow to attain greater focus and concentration.

Tip #1: Follow the five ____ rule.

There will be instances that you feel like you're unable to concentrate on your task for any longer. You'll decide to stop or postpone tasks until the following day, or even the next week. When you're in this situation the best thing to do is follow the five-minute rule.

Which is the Five additional rules?

This rule is quite easy to follow. It is a way to encourage you to go through five more pages of that boring manuscript or draw five additional pages in your comic book as well as listen to 5 interviews recorded and so on.

When you're feeling tired or simply unfocused, you should give yourself a deadline. You may decide to quit your job after you've used the five-minute rule, or not quit completely.

The goal is that when you're finished with the additional five pages, sketches or interviews recorded you'll be able to regain your determination and focus to finish the entire project. If not, at least you've achieved a small amount of progress, which is always better than the absence of anything.

TIP #2: Utilize start-stop-time parameters.

The majority of people perform better and are more focused on their jobs when they have the same beginning and ending time. It is possible to use these hours to increase your focus too.

If, for instance, you have edit an essay about the life of the English Royalty Give you 60 minutes to complete the job. You must be sure of your choices. When you begin the 60-minute timer, it will gradually diminish. Your brain will need to complete the task in the quickest time possible. The next time you're faced with lots of things to finish, assign each one a start-to-stop time and then watch your list become shorter and shorter.

Tip #3: Blow your brain.

As surprising as it may be, bribery can work with respect to the brain. If you have difficulty concentration or concentrating on a single task at a given time then give your brain a greater motivation to do the task at hand.

You can reward yourself with easy rewards for doing simple tasks as well as more expensive rewards to complete more complex tasks. For instance, you could say that for each HTML website that you code you get to eat one scoop of ice-cream after work. That means that if you code three HTML websites, you are entitled three scoops of ice-cream. It might sound a bit childish however this method has been tested by experts and novices. The brain is awe-inspiring when it's stimulated, and the thought of a reward at close of a tough day's work can give you all the motivation you require to keep your focus.

Tips #4: Do not try to cram Don't delay, and don't be a procrastinator.

If you've got something that you're required to complete take action right now. Today, when you're not distracted. Make sure you are busy and free from distractions the longest time you can. Be aware that trying to squeeze in your work will not help you in the long run. Simply get at your workstation, studio or office and get started today. Don't wait or in less than five minutes, not even after watching one show on Netflix But now.

Tip #5 Tip #5: Multitasking is not a fact.

Eliminate the practice of completing many tasks at once. This isn't the case. In reality, you are able to take on several projects and work on one at a time, and then move to another and the cycle continues. It is impossible to do two things simultaneously as well as three, or even four. What's that? You say you can multitask?

Let's clear it up. What's happening when you are trying at multitasking is it forces your brain to be focused on several things at once. Sometimes , this is effective however most of the time , you'll end up creating mediocre outputs or you'll get an awful headache and not get all of your chores completed. Don't be distracted. Make sure you are completing only one task at a given time, while building your ability to pay attention and to stay focused.

TIP #6: Have a moment to rest every now and again.

Contrary to what many believe, taking a break every now and again can actually boost your concentration. Reenergize yourself during the course of a stressful day lowers the stress levels and helps you stay motivated to complete your tasks.

After you're done with an assignment or two you've completed, take five minutes to relax, go through a chapter from your favourite book, or draw a sketch to relax your hands. Have a break every now and then , and return to work more productive than ever before.

Tip #7: Be careful not to fall victim to distractions. Disconnect the Internet connection if your job does not have anything to do with research online or social media.

Switch off the TV and turn off the radio.

Clear your desk.

Make sure you keep your work just your job, in your sight. The main reason for distractions is that to-do lists don't work. Don't let them be the top of your list. agenda. Get them killed as soon as you can.

Tipp #8: Have a restful night's rest.

If you're looking to improve your focus on your work, then take more care of yourself. A lot of people in the workplace are unable to focus on their work because they couldn't get enough rest. Let your brain relax and recharge. You should get at minimum six hours of rest each day. You should also get eight hours of sleep whenever you are able to.

Tips #9: Food is important also.

That's right. Even if you've had enough rest, but you ate junk foodor, worse than that, you ate absolutely nothing, then the odds of staying focused throughout the day are extremely low. Get healthy. Make sure you are eating healthy foods to boost your body and brain. There's no way anyone would like to be sick. And nobody can be innovative and efficient if the body or mind aren't adequately fed.

Tip #10 Do not forget to surround yourself with positive, focused people.

When you surround yourself with people who are focused or driven to reach the top, you will be in a position to learn their ideas. You are a part of their synergy and, of course you'll wish to emulate their style also. If you are able pick your officemates with care. Select the people you would like to become like one day and remain close to them.

Chapter 13: The Laws Of Attraction, Polarity And Negative Beliefs

You could be attracted to more negative situations because of your negative beliefs despite your best efforts to be focused on the things you really want. If you continue to set your mind against the deeply-rooted negative beliefs that you hold in your subconscious, you may be making yourself vulnerable to receiving more negative circumstances. To be able to overcome negative thoughts, you need to understand what your Law of Attraction and Polarity combine along with the beliefs you hold to shape your reality.

Your subconscious mind and the role it plays. The incredibly powerful mental programs that govern all aspects that you live are carried out through your unconscious mind. Your conscious mind doesn't have to play a role in this process. It is entirely controlled in your mind's subconscious. Positive and negative beliefs, the emotional vibrations and habits of your actions, as well as your general mindset and the circumstances that you live in are what the mental programming is based on.

Negative Beliefs What Are they? They limit your

beliefs in all aspects of your life and prevent you from reaching your goals. The beliefs you hold are the primary aspect in creating your own reality. Your source of habitual beliefs is believed to be the power of your thoughts which is at the core of your conscious creation. It has a significant impact on your perception of reality. Your personal beliefs and positive beliefs are the basis of your success , but your negative beliefs can hinder your success.

Your subconscious mind is serving Your Success. Your subconscious mind will use the programs you've given it but is unable to differentiate between the negative and positive beliefs that you hold. Also, it doesn't know which software will be most beneficial to you for your achievement. It's not enthusiastic about altering programs but that doesn't mean you can't alter your subconscious mind, however it isn't easy to attain. It is possible to get rid of negative beliefs by changing your concentration.
Your emotional vibration must be in sync with your new mental focus. The fact that you have new focus on your mind does not necessarily mean you're subconsciously aware or that your emotional vibrations are yet. Your subconscious

needs time mind to adjust to the changes in your emotions. Your negative beliefs affect what you believe about the Law of Attraction to understand this better , it is important to examine the role in your Law of Polarity in creating your life circumstances.

The Law of Polarity. This Law of Polarity is one of the Seven Universal Laws it tells us that everything is dual. It implies the two elements that appear to be in opposition actually are different levels of the identical thing. One simple illustration is the fact that We think of them as opposing concepts, however in reality, they are two distinct kinds from the exact same concept, which is why we call temperature. This is the case when you're trying to manifest something within your own life. You can't be wealthy without also having the other spectrum , which is less as it is with the same package. you cannot get one with the opposite. It is impossible to attract a healthy body without the ability to draw a body that is unhealthy.

The Laws of Attraction and Polarity work together. It is said that the Laws of Attraction state that you attract to yourself the things you're in alignment with and also what you are thinking about. In The Law of Polarity it states that everything is dual , and that what appears to be two extremes which appear to be in opposition, but they however they are actually inseparable. This means that you'll be drawn to the entire array of thoughts but you'll manifest the portion of the package which you are in harmonious with. If you focus on what you don't think you currently have because of your negative beliefs, your subconscious might think that you are seeking more of the things is already yours. If you are struggling with a lack of funds, for example, and you claim that you want your financial situation to improve, your subconscious could interpret this as a desire for more money problems. If your vibration in the emotional realm is one of desperation, it will draw additional of the same. There is a way to overcome negative beliefs and be in alignment to the Laws of Attraction and Polarity so that you are in a position to manifest the things you want, instead of having the same things you don't desire.

Let's first look at the times what you need to be focusing on when it comes to the things you'd like to achieve.

The right time to focus on the Things You Want. It is possible to begin to concentrate on something you desire right away, provided you don't already have negative beliefs regarding it. One way to determine whether you've got an existing negative view of your goals is to determine if you're currently experiencing the opposite results of what you would like to see in your life. Most likely, you have a negative belief in connection with the goal you wish to attain.

Positive Beliefs Are Powerful. It is possible to focus on the positive thoughts of your subconscious mind to ensure that you be more attracted to these positive thoughts in accordance with your Laws of Attraction and Polarity. If, for instance, you're an active and healthy individual and you're contemplating running a long race, you can focus your mind and imagine yourself completing the race. If you're a professional who is successful but are looking to boost your sales, try focusing on the satisfaction of having more sales.

Being aware of when to not focus on what you want. If your belief system is positive, it is only natural that you should be focusing on the positive aspect of your belief. If it's an untruthful belief, that you are not able to focus on your goals.

Try The By-Product Method. If you're trying to get rid of an unhelpful belief by using concentration, the By-Product Method is a fantastic method of accomplishing this. When you use this method, you focus your attention on the by-product of what you really would like to achieve. For instance, if you're an author and you want to earn $100,000 annually to support your writing career , but you are unable to focus on this because there are negative thoughts in your mind about this subject. Instead, you could concentrate on the result of this like writing a bestseller romantic novel.

Positive Beliefs can be changed through a By-Product Image. Your beliefs are also subject to the Law of Polarity. For each of your negative beliefs , you have your positive belief.

If you keep putting your attention on a product image, without paying attention to the part of it you want to see, your mind's subconscious can quickly and effortlessly allow negative thoughts to be transformed into positive ones. It is possible to keep your subconscious brain occupied by focusing on an image that is free of negative thought while changing the negative beliefs that do not match the new positive image of the by-product. The things you attract and what you create within your life will be determined by your concentration. Focusing on only your desires, it could result in a derailment of the effort to make your ideal reality. This happens most often when you believe in a negative idea that is the basis of your goals. If you concentrate on something that is based on an unfavourable belief, chances are you'll get an even greater amount of it. If you are able to concentrate your mind on the outcome of what you want to achieve, it will prevent your mind's subconscious from fighting your mind's focus. This helps to guarantee a positive results you desire.

Chapter 14: Grounding To Support Meditation And Visualization

One thing that I've noticed is it is that many people do not explain that grounding is an essential element in meditation or visualization. Anyone who is familiar with meditation or visualization is aware of this as an essential aspect of the procedure.

This is the first step you must do prior to beginning meditation or visualisation. If you were to think of an air balloon that wasn't fixed to the ground, you'd just be floating and would never be grounded and well-balanced.

It's like wandering around. One of the most fascinating facts I've learnt about grounded is that it keeps me grounded and focused.

Even if I was climbing a mountain or cliff, I'd still need an anchor to prevent me from falling backwards to the bottom of the mountain.

Grounding provides stability and keeps us from becoming the air and flying.

There are a variety of methods for the practice of grounding and methods. The best method to begin any type of meditation or practice is to shut your eyes. You can lie down or lie in an armchair.

What is the most comfortable option for you? There isn't a proper or incorrect method of meditation.

It is possible to perform this exercise in the morning , when you wake up, or after you are ready to go to sleep. It can be done virtually anywhere at any time. In your car, in the bathroom, at work at home, even outside.

Find a quiet spot in which you are sure you won't be distracted. Switch off your cellphone, the computer or any other device that is distracting. Some people do this using gentle music while some do not listen to any kind of music. Each person's style of music is unique. Be sure that there aren't any animals children, pets, or people in the area so that you won't be at risk of being disturbed.

When you are thinking about your thoughts allow them to flow naturally. It's not wise to fight them , or even fight against your mind. Recognize them whenever they appear and then let them go. Meditation is a process that lasts for a lifetime and the more you develop the habit of doing it every day, the more effective and efficient you'll get over time.

Start with one day at a time , and let yourself get used to the concept of the practice of meditation.

There's no reason for you to feel anxious or stressed out. It could take anywhere from up to 6 months to become familiar with the process and proficient in your ability to focus.

Set yourself a time limit to begin with five to 10 minutes each and gradually build up to making longer and longer lengths of time.

It starts by grounding through sending the energy cord downwards to your chakra's red and also the ovaries or testicles. The energy chord must be grounded to the core in the Earth.

Another option is to imagine yourself lying in a field of bright tulips and feeling roots sinking into the dark soils of earth, spreading out and securing your. Enjoy the soft petals and smell the scent that is bursting out of the air. The earth is firmly hugging you with pure love.

Another way to imagine you're an oak tree that's sturdy and sturdy. Imagine the powerful roots of this tree spread its their roots across the ground beneath the earth. Imagine mother earth giving you a bath in mud and eliminating all the negative energy out of your life. It purifies your heart, skin as well as every cell and every muscle of your body.

After you've established your grounding however

you want to then you're ready to proceed to meditation and visualization.

Relax Your Body Visualization Allow your body to let your body relax. Your hands and arms can rest on your side or rest on your heart chakra, folded or even on your knees. Be sure to wear clothes that feel comfortable and not too tight.

Take a deep breath and be in the moment and feel the sensation. Try to remain in the moment and not think. If you are having any, let them enter and let them roll away as waves gently reach the shoreline of the lake.

Slowly, waves come in and out one after another. Every thought should move in the same direction as the tides. Every emotion must move between forward and reverse, and inward and outward. Allow yourself to take a break for a couple of minutes. You're completely free to live at your own pace and at your own pace. There is no place for you to be at this point in time. There is nothing that you need to do at this specific moment.

Your mind could wander to other thoughts, but you must bring your attention back to the moment in which you are.

Breathe deep. Breathe into positive energy. Breathe in the love energy. Inhale the negative energy, and exhale anger energy. Repeat this process three to five times in succession.

You will feel at home in a soft space. You're in a secure area in which no one will ever hurt or harm you. This is your own personal location, and nobody else has access to this space only you. Get rid of any notions about what you ought to do or not. Let yourself be who you are. Let the experience flow effortlessly. Relax at your own pace and in the way that feels comfortable to you.

Imagine yourself sitting on an island with a heart shape. The only emotion or feeling you'll experience is love. The only thing you can feel is love. Breathe deeply in love.

The sapphire sky is adorned in white, puffy clouds floating in a row. They're so soft and fluffy. The clouds appear inviting and warm as you gaze up at the sky. See the clouds transform into hearts of love.

The waves of the ocean are quiet and calm. The water is crystal clear , and you can see depths of ocean. Step into the warm waters and let the sunlight gently stroke your cheeks with a rosy glow. The water is relaxing and refreshing on your skin.

It is a relaxing experience to sink into the sparkling surface and lay on your head. You drift away as the water gently holds you and gently cradles you in love.

There is a sound of seagulls flying over. It is easy to see them spread their wings while they glide over the skyline of sapphire. You are relaxed when you relax and relax.

There are two white swans close by. Slowly , you begin to swim towards them.

Enjoy every stroke as you move towards them, getting closer.

You are five yards away from the Swans. You can see how pure and white the swans appear.

Take note of how gorgeous they are moving in the lake in perfect unison. Then you rise from the warm water to the shoreline of the lake and watch them move along in the sun's rays.

Take one of the soft swan feathers that are lying on the ground. Be aware of the top of the feather as well as the tiny small pieces of slivers that make the shape. Smile with the point of it. See the smile on your face get brighter.

Smiling feels wonderful. It is easy to feel glow of love inside your heart. Feel your heart warm from being surrounded by the love of your life.

Swans remind us how wonderful it is to be in harmony and peace with nature. Enjoy the radiant sunshine warming your body.

Let yourself be filled with the most love you can. Allow love to radiate from the entirety of your being. It will enhance your positive qualities. Keep in mind that love is a wonderful experience.

You can hold this state for as long as you'd like. When you're ready for the end of your meditation, you can anytime.

Open your eyes. Take a few moments to relax and then think about the meditation and let your body get back to your normal.

Island Visualization

Let your body relax. The hands and arms could be placed on your sides, the heart chakra can be folded, or even on your knees. Make sure that you're wearing clothes that feel comfortable and aren't too tight.

Shut your eyes, and take in the experience. Try to remain in the moment without thoughts. If you do have any thoughts, let them enter and then let them go like waves that gently sway towards the shoreline of the lake.

Slowly, waves come in and out one at a time. Every thought should move in the same direction as the tides. Every emotion should move both ways, forward and backward, inside and outward. Allow yourself to relax for a couple of minutes. You're free to be at your own pace and at your own pace. There is nothing to do at this point in time. There's nothing you need to accomplish at this particular moment.

Your mind could wander to other thoughts, but keep your attention back to the moment in which you are.

Breathe deep. Breathe into positive energy. Breathe in the love energy. Inhale the negative energy, and exhale anger energy. Repeat this process three to five times in succession.

You will feel at home in a and cosy space. You're now in a safe space that no one could ever hurt or harm you. This is your personal location, and nobody else is able to access it except you.

Get rid of any notions about what you ought to experience or should not have to experience. Be yourself. Let the experience flow effortlessly. Relax at your own pace and in the way that feels comfortable to you.

Imagine yourself on an island of sand, far away from the daily routine. Feel the sand slide in between the toes of your feet. Take a step back as you feel tiny sand grains move through your fingers.

Take a walk to the north , through those palms. Take a look at how long and lush the palm leaves are as well as their swaying shade over your head that blocks the sun's rays.

Take a stroll through the endless forest of palms. Pay attention to their unique sizes and shapes. Enjoy the air of summer blow against you.

Step into the long dock, and meet the pelican which is perched on the edge. In the quiet, the pelican is looking at you. Enjoy the tranquil moment. Be gentle when approaching. Look at how gorgeous she appears with her black and white feathers.

You can remain still and in a solitary position and enjoy the beauty of her experience. There is no one scared. You are safe and relaxed when you greet each other.

Check out her flaps of wings as she lifts off into the sky and ends her flight. Watch her wings spread out over the pastel sky.

Take a seat into the wooden canoe and grasp the paddle. Then, you can paddle off from the dock and into endless miles of peaceful lapis water. Coast along the waterfall. Be aware of the water's roaring as you drop into the waters below while you continue to paddle upstream. The water

pools in a circular pattern below the waterfall.
In the distance, up ahead you can see dolphins jumping and from the sea. You take a break from paddling and lie back to watch the dolphins. Their echos talk at you with their own language.
They're stunning when they come up to your canoe, and then meet you at the point of their noses to welcome you.
It's a fantastic experience as they welcome you in to the world of their. Then you paddle to the north, leaving the dolphins in their wake. Then you stop at a huge rock. You climb up and gaze at the stunning landscape. The mountains are stunning in the background of the palm trees that are tall. The water is calm and soothing to the senses.
You lie in the rock, and extend your legs. Your body is relaxed and relaxed as you lay in the sunshine. Every muscle that is tight now is loose, not tight.
Your breathing is slow and deep. Your mind is absorbed by the waves. You can smell the fresh white orchids that are close to you. The scent awakens your nose. The waves splash against the rocks and you kiss the tops of your toes with an easy splash.
Drink from the small coconut and feel energized.

The birds chirp in the back of those palms, while the gentle beat of the drums pound gently with your heart.

You're blissfully happy to be free of anxieties and worries. Your day was refreshed by spending a few moments to be a part of Mother Nature. You've had a wonderful time with wildlife and it has blessed you with affection.

You can hold this state for as long as you'd like. If you're ready to stop your meditation, you can at any point.

Simply open your eyes. You can take a few minutes to unwind and then contemplate the experience and let your body get back to your normal.

Chapter 15: Tips To Increase Your Creativity

New research suggests the way to a variety of ecological and mental methods that will allow us to improve our productivity and innovation:

1. Utilize the counterfactual approach

Counterfactual thinking, or asking "What might have been?" is proven to boost creativity in short periods of time. To investigate different possibilities for this approach, look at events which have already occurred and think about different outcomes using a mix of the subtractive mental model (taking parts of the event) as well as the additive approach (adding factors to the event).

An absurd example of counterfactual thought in action can be observed in The Big Bang Theory, where one of the principal characters participates in the wonder, and asks his flatmate: "In a world where Rhinoceroses are pets that can be controlled Who will win this Second World War?" But, you could apply this to more real-world scenarios, such as drawing out the results at whatever moment you're engaging in creative critical thinking, removing or adding "what would happen" factors that would influence the outcome.

2. Re-conceptualize the problem

Experts have observed that creative people tend to think about problems more frequently before beginning the task of their imagination. For example, as Einstein once stated "If I had an time limit of an hour to address an issue , I'd spend 55 minutes of thinking about the problem and five minutes thinking about possible arrangements." Instead of focusing on the ultimate goal of an imaginative project (i.e. "I must create an outstanding painting") It's better to consider the subject from different, more significant edges prior to starting ("What kind of artwork will bring back the feelings of sadness that everyone feels following a breakup? ").

The most effective method is to imagine the crowd for your next project. What motivates them? What are they bored of having to hear about? What are the challenges they face, but every now and then they're willing to discuss?

3. Be astonished by your achievements

I've discovered my favourite music through listening to professional performers and also by finding out whom they are listening to. With no fizzle, amazing artists are watching incredible artists and great artists look at amazing artists. It is essential to always learn and be in contact with amazing art, incredible literature, amazing music and most importantly, amazing people. This will give you the form of quality and excellence which can propel your imagination ahead.

There's nothing wrong when you study and even copying the best of your field. For example, Pablo Picasso once said, "Great artists copy, great artists learn." While I am in agreement with Picasso but it's not saying that you must follow their approach and not their products.

I'm sure that you're familiar with the verbal structure which allows you to think about something with one hand and the other. This is a unique method because of its ability to allows us to think about an exam from multiple perspectives.

This is amazing. Researchers have discovered that when you raise one hand and then raise the other hand, you'll come up with much better ideas than if you stood with one hand by itself. The researchers propose that this fundamental behavior is an indication to the brain that it is required to examine the subject from multiple angles.

4. Don't pay attention to the Scoffers

Creativity has to be shared. But, this puts the artist in an unreliable condition, subject to criticism and scrutiny. In the realm of games, business and other expressions of personal experience of humans, and even in life generally speaking, you'll encounter critics who are sour and who think they have the ability to grow through pushing you down (you may be your own most critical critic).

Be open to suggestions and changes from people who are in your best interests on a fundamental level however, you should not allow any space to an insulting comment.

Don't be a scoffer and, better yet, use their negative comments as source of inspiration. Every amazing creative person was criticized by critics who said they weren't good enough, but the past doesn't remember the reviews, but rather the imagination, inspiration, creativity and creativity.

5. Going for an outing

I'm sure that you've had the impression that sitting on the case might have sparked your thoughts a little and this scenario is a little less shocking. It's widely known that walking, as well as other kinds of exercise can be beneficial for your mind.

The study revealed that you can boost your imagination when you walk in a certain method. Researchers pushed people to complete a task by taking a square-shaped walk as opposed to walking randomly. Surprisingly, the random wanderers won the race.

6. Develop Your Creative Potential

The first step is to commit yourself to the development of your imaginative capabilities. Do not put off your work. Set goals, solicit help from others and schedule time every day to improve your skills.

7. Reward Your Curiosity

One of the biggest obstacles in the development of creativity is the belief that curiosity is an over-indulgence. Instead of criticizing yourself, praise yourself whenever you're intrigued by something. Allow yourself to learn about new topics.

While it is essential to reward yourself but it's also crucial to generate intrinsic inspiration. Every now and then the true reward of creative thinking is the process rather than the result.

8. Sleep

This is the time where your brain creates information and organizes all the information that is circulating around your brain. If you awake and are astonished by the ideas that pop in your head!

9. Assemble Your Confidence

A lack of confidence in your abilities could hinder creativity This is why it's important to establish confidence. Take note of the progress you've made, appreciate your accomplishments and always be vigilant for ways to boost your creative flair.

10. Find the time to be creative

It's impossible to increase your creative gifts if you don't allocate time to do these. Schedule a time each week to devote to something creative.

11. You can ask questions about your situation.

Take a piece of paper, an electronic scratch pad, laptop or any other device you can use to record notes and then ask questions on your an area of interest. It's likely that you'll see ideas coming out once you've completed this.

12. Overcome negative attitudes that block creativity.

According to a report released in Proceedings of the National Academy of Sciences Positive mind-sets can boost your ability to think ingenuously. Based on Professor Dr. Adam Anderson, senior researcher of this research "If your job requires you to be innovative or being in a thinking tank, you should be on an excellent mindset." Be sure to eliminate negative thoughts or self-criticisms which could harm your ability to build good imaginative skills.

13. Exercise your brain

Like bodies, brains require exercise to remain in good shape. If you don't work out your brain it will become inactive and unproductive. Train your mind by studying a lot amount (see above) and conversing with intelligent people, and debating with others - arguing could be a great way for giving your brain cells exercise. It is important to note that debates about the film industry or politics can be good for you, but arguing over who is the best person to wash the dishes is not.

14. Brainstorm to come up with new ideas

Brainstorming is an everyday practice for professional and academic environments, but it can also be an effective tool to develop your imagination. Start by letting go of your judgement and self-criticism, and then start writing down your ideas and potential solutions. The goal is to come up with the most diverse ideas you can in a short period of time. After that, focus on defining and refining your thoughts so that you can arrive on the best option.

15. Make mind maps

Mind maps are tools that encourage users to record each and every thing that can be associated with a specific concept or word. They're also extremely useful charts, great to help you organize your twisted thoughts and tackling seemingly daunting problems. When you create an outline of your mind, you allow your brain to draw out all the possible options and possible scenarios, a method that can get your creative flow going for years.

16. Keep a Creativity Journal

Begin to keep a diary to record your creative method and record the concepts that you come up with. It is a fantastic way to look back at the work you've done and look for alternatives to your current ways to organize your thoughts. It can also be used to record ideas that could be used later on as ideas.

17. Challenge yourself to think differently and find opportunities to be creative.

If you've developed the basic abilities to think creatively it is essential to keep moving forward to increase your capabilities. Find more challenging methods and try out new ideas and avoid employing the same strategies that you've been using in the past.

As well as trying new things, you have to create your own unique opportunities to be creative. This might mean taking on a different project or finding new methods to apply in your current tasks.

18. Stop Doing Drugs

I'm talking about processed drinks, food, and cigarettes. It's not necessary to remind you to take any hard drugs! Your health will benefit in the long run, and you'll feel a lot quantity more energetic. There is a good chance that you'll find many new sources of motivation that is accompanied by your new health levels when you start eating well and avoiding garbage.

19. Look for Inspirational Sources

Do not expect that creative thinking happens naturally. Find new sources of inspiration, which will offer you fresh concepts and prompt you to think of creative responses to questions. Read a book, go to an exhibition space or listen to your favourite music, or participate in a lively and spirited discussion with your partner. Utilize the method or strategy that is most effective for you.

20. Find Something You Enjoy

Are you stuck for ideas? Are you unsure of how to proceed? Your life requires some balance to ensure your imagination doesn't last forever.

In a letter addressed to his son, Albert Einstein gave an amazing piece of fatherly wisdom in addressing his child's curiosity in the piano. It is pertinent to losing yourself in the process of creating to accomplish something that pleases you.

"That is how you get the most from your education, is when you do something you love so much that you forget that time is passing," Einstein wrote. "I often get so caught with my job that I do not think about lunch"

Creative and affection are linked. The pursuit of leisure like taking a musical instrument to the stage, or running or collecting memorabilia, could help you with the stress of battle and relaxation while also giving your creative side help.

21. Solve riddles of parallel thinking

While the typical riddles will stimulate your brain but it's the thinking riddles that provide an even more challenging test. To answer this kind of puzzle, you have use an imaginative and indirect method to arrive with a variety of possible solutions. While there may be a myriad of answers to a problem that requires parallel thinking but there's usually only one that makes most sense. The use of the traditional orderly logic isn't normally useful in this type of puzzle, which makes the puzzle more difficult and stimulating for creativity.

22. Make the Right Mood

A lack of thought or an insignificant approach to the treatment of a problem can be to a significant extent frustrating.

If you don't like complete silence music could be an ideal way to provide your mindset, as well as your creativity, a helping hand. Steve Jobs utilized music to change his mood and stay creative. It can work for you, too.

23. Take it easy on yourself

Stop criticizing yourself and stop self-pitying about yourself. Accept yourself for who you are and work at the highest level of abilities. You are enough and you are creative. Do not let your self-limiting beliefs block your creative ideas! Leave the boundaries, and your ideas will flow.

24. Choose a terrible idea

Get away from the notion you've been stuck with for a few minutes.

What's the most useless idea you can think of? List the most absurd ideas you could come up with. The real test is to increase your creative thinking is to ask yourself What are the most effective aspects of these terrible ideas. Perhaps looking at these disgusting concepts will inspire you to think of something new which you can transfer into your creative thought.

25. Create a list and choose your ideas

Sometimes, the exact opposite of an imaginative square occurs - you have too many ideas! Although it's fantastic but it could also leave you feel overwhelmed. You can organize your thoughts by keeping a notepad. Note down each thought that ring an alarm and decide the one you believe is the most effective. It is also possible to carry an eraser and a small scratch pads wherever you go, so that you keep your thoughts that pop up while riding a bus eating lunch, studying books or watching videos on the internet.

26. Utilize the the peak hours

Certain individuals are more creative and effective in specific times during the day whereas others are more inventive in the depth of their thoughts. Get your heart pumping during these times , and let your creative creativity flow freely. The ability to be creative can also be enhanced by putting yourself in a particular area in the room or surround yourself in certain songs. The process of releasing creativity differs on a different level from person to. There's a firm rule of thumb for the time of day or the atmosphere around you should be in to experience a sense of wonder. Just do what is best for you.

27. Relax

Creative thinking and smart ideas typically do not manifest under stress. If you're relaxed and reenergized, innovative ideas tend to appear more often. Get a sigh of fresh air on the beach, take part in some activity or whatever else relaxes your mind, so that you is more creative when you get back to work.

28. Find out how you learn best.

Some people may prefer to maintain their entire point of view in their head; other may prefer to keep their thoughts off of others or even objects that are inanimate by expressing themselves verbally, while others prefer to draw mind maps and then write down what's going on in their heads. Learn through the various tests that are available, like for instance, the Kolb as well as the Honey and Mumford tests which one is going to aid you the most. not just follow what other people do because their heads function in a different way than yours! It's about making the most of you.

29. Paint the town blue , not red

Concentrates on have demonstrated that the blue

color produces twice as much profit as the red color on creative tasks. In contrast, the color red is more powerful in improving tender love blue will assist both you and your mind achieve that magic touch that can bring about a huge difference to you. Get your hands on some blue ink pens and decorate your workplace with images of the ocean to give your brain all you can.

Chapter 16: Prevention Of Self-Consciousness Excessive

If you're self-conscious, it has the tendency to fill your thoughts with negative ones. You'd think that people have been talking to you about yourself, but in reality, they're just going about their lives. Even if they are, you need to accept that it's like that and people will always be able to talk about you, so it's best to simply live your day. It's not easy to feel confident and eliminate these thoughts out of your mind, however, you can attempt. Here are some strategies to avoid becoming self-conscious and to feel more confident in crowds:

1. Be aware that self-consciousness isn't a good thing. When you're self-conscious you don't see the beauty in the situation, and instead think that others will be critical of you or that people will hate you. This can put you in a negative mood immediately and of course, it makes you think that you need to hide from the world or should not even try to interact with people.

In addition, being self-conscious causes you to forget other aspects of the event and you concentrate on the negatives. Then, you lose details. That's not ideal because, sometimes the appeal of an event lies in the details. You also need to consider the fact that there are many people looking to get you.

2. Change perspectives. The reason you're self-conscious is because you observe the world around you in a an illuminating way that you feel people have negative opinions about you, or they're trying to judge your behavior.

Why don't you reflect on how you think instead? Concentrate upon your thought process. It is a good idea to practice this in public transportation , or perhaps even in a room filled with people. Take a look at how you view other people. Find out what's currently troubling you. Stop considering that others are trying to see your presence or are observing you. You're not being observed by the microscope.

Then, begin a conversation with any person you see, particularly those who smiled at you , made a greeting or similar. In doing this you will be aware that not everyone is identical and there are many people who are looking to harm or judge you.

3. Smile! It's such a cliché but the fact is, when you smile, other people are likely to smile too, or something like that. The act of smiling can break down a lot of barriers due to it being an easy, but

huge flashing neon signal of friendship. When you smile you establish a quick bond between yourself and your friend and that can help you begin having conversations with each other. When you're talking, remember to smile. Smile as you talk and it aids in speaking your messages in an easy manner, so that there's less tension. It can be difficult to look someone else at eye level in case you suffer from social anxiety which is why smiling could be a good option. Even if you don't glance at them directly the expression will be visible.

4. You can watch TV or films. It's not about making you look like couch potato, but rather about watching actors perform various characters. No you don't need to be an arrogant person, however, by watching these actors and the scenarios they're placed in, you'll also be able to comprehend what you are able to perform in these specific circumstances so that you don't become insecure. In this way, if you're going to be looking at youfrom afar, it's bound be treated as some kind of way.

Practice by looking at yourself in the mirror and performing a scene or two. You can also pretend you're in a video. It might be awkward initially, but sooner and later you'll get grasp of it. It's a great method of building confidence and to see yourself in as others might consider you.

5. Try to focus your attention on the outside. Focusing on the outside is observing the people who are around you. Is this a sign that you are gossipy? No. It's simply a method of placing yourself in other people's shows because you already know that they speak and consider you, so this is an opportunity to observe them as well. Pay attention to how they talk and the way their bodies or hands move during speaking and attempt to learn a lesson or two from them, even when you don't actually speak to them. It's a method to gain "revenge" inside your head without ever being a villain.

6. Prepare yourself. Being self-conscious can be stressful enough, however if you're that kind that goes through life unprepared, then are likely to have plenty of worries about.

One of the reasons the majority of people feel conscious of their appearance is the fact that they realize that they're doing things at a sloppy level. They're not putting in a lot of effort. If you're aware that you're well-prepared for what you need to accomplish, such as an presentation or speech, you're sure that you'll be able to impress the audience. If you're well-prepared then you'll have less things to think about. 7. Remember: Damned if are doing it, but damned if do not. The legendary Eleanor Roosevelt was right when she stated that. But what do you know? Whatever your actions, someone is going to be saying something.

It is impossible to satisfy everybody. Certain people will be critical of them simply because they want to. Certain people not see the positive aspects of you because they're too critical. However, there will be those who appreciate the person you are.

Social anxiety and feeling self-conscious can make it difficult to realize this. But it is important to recognize that if you dwell on negative thoughts and do not strive to improve yourself, you're only hurting yourself. Don't be a 'people pleaser' as it is going to harm your soul.

Chapter 17: Procrastination Stagnation, And Personal Growth:

Does Personal Development Really Worth the Cost?

As we've seen that personal development is a way to motivate yourself toward personal achievement. Procrastination and stagnation are both self-defeating characteristics. Self-defeating, in the sense that no matter how gorgeous or stunning your "dream life" appears until you decide to get rid of these two character flaws within your own life, your "imagined ideal life' will be only that, an imagined.

We've previously mentioned that there are numerous ways to beat stagnation and procrastination. Personal development is the top priority on the list. It is possible that you are wondering what is the effectiveness of personal growth?

So, here's the solution. The creative visualization that you did earlier highlighted personal growth, it is the way towards a more fulfilled self. Personal development is a paradigm shift , and is the exact opposite of stagnation and procrastination. Be aware that procrastination can be a negative energy whereas stagnation is not energy in any way (meaning that the self is subject to the influence of other energies, most of which have negative energy).

If you decide to embark on your personal development path or process, you're choosing to become a positive-motivated lighting rod (when you're optimistic and a fundamental principle of personal success and success, you're more likely to receive positive lightening blasts of light from all directions). Positive energy is the catalyst for positive change within your life.

Though we've mentioned it earlier in passing The law of attraction says that similar energy attracts like energy and you will become what you think about constantly. Static and procrastination are negative energy and therefore cannot be within the same container (you) for personal growth because the former has positive energy.

Personal growth has a positive impact on all the pillars in your daily life. By choosing to follow the personal development track, you're likely to end procrastination and stagnation as the pursuit of personal excellence is often the seeds of enthusiasm and motivation.

What we have been able to see so far: personal growth is certainly worth the effort and we should all take it seriously. Personal development gives you the knowledge and motivation you require to realize your dream that you imagined through the creative visualization exercises we did earlier.

Personal development or motivation for personal improvement is the shovel and boost that you need to take you from being ordinary to exceptional. It is ultimately the genie that you have been looking for when you want to step out of the monotony of your daily life and reach the new level of achievement in every endeavor.

To be positive, we must transformation and as we have said earlier Personal growth and development isn't a single thing by itself. For instance this Wikipedia source states that personal growth is the process of increasing self-knowledge, increasing self-awareness, increasing wealth, spiritual growth and achieving goals, among other things.

While this book is extensive in its efforts to describe the various areas that personal development covers however, it doesn't make a point the fact that personal growth can be different and show up differently for different individuals.

In addition it is important to note that you may

choose to utilize personal development to improve or improve a specific aspect that you are living in. For instance, although personal development may work with other aspects of your life, you could choose to apply personal growth and development to attain peace and harmony in your spiritual life or to improve your physical and mental health.

I hope this chapter has demonstrated to that you need to be consistent in your personal growth and also provides several ways in that personal growth can help you break out and from a rut or procrastination.

Since this course is about how to utilize self-development and motivation to reach your new level of accomplishment, the remaining part of this book is going to focus on how you can use motivation and personal development to attain your next level of achievement in various areas of your life.

Setting Goals is the epitome of self-growth: How to Design Smart, Achievable Goals
In the past, we have discussed some of the causes that our lives are stagnant. We also discussed the various reasons why we should not be averse to

stagnation or procrastination , despite it being a beautiful, glimmering bed.

We also discussed the personal growth aspect. We defined what that means and then discussed ways it can assist you in taking back your control over your life. In doing so we also stated that personal growth is your goal, desire, and active engagement towards becoming the best you can be.

One thing we talked about is the courage you have to start and your drive to continue despite the stagnation bed and procrastination entices and teases you to will invite you to join them. Let's face it for a second If you're here or something similar, it's probably because your life seems a little slow or it seems to be a little monotonous and you'd like to change it. What nobody else will explain to you as you browse through the many personal motivational books that you can get online or offline; personal motivation isn't something that can be found in books. Books can certainly inspire and offer suggestions regarding how to achieve your goals, but they can't make the choice for you. What is the best choice?

"The choice to improve or to continuously strive for personal excellence"

The first step to stepping from your comfortable zone or stagnation, or getting rid of procrastination, is to make the choice to start working towards becoming the best version of yourself you can be. The best method to accomplish this is to set goals.

We will not specify the definition of goals. However, we will emphasize is how important it is to set them and continuously striving to achieve them both consciously and subconsciously. Setting goals is an important element of personal growth. Also, as we've observed, personal growth is the an effort to achieve personal excellence. In the absence of setting goals or actively working towards those goals (remember that pursuit is a aware, i.e. any action that's geared toward the accomplishment to goals or unconscious i.e. employing your mind's subconscious to create desired goals) Your life will be stagnant , and you are likely to be afflicted by procrastination.

How can procrastination manifest itself? It manifests in the form of a myriad of unfinished projects and a scattershot approach to the achievement of life's goals, all designed to bring you the life you want' as illustrated in the exercise of creative visualization that we had previously practiced. To be able to live the life you wish for you must set goals that will lead you towards your goal of living the life you want and to be actively working towards those goals.

For instance, if you want to utilize personal development to reduce procrastination and rid your life of stagnation, it is necessary to establish goals that push you to the opposite of the current circumstance. One good illustration is when your life is a little dull and boring.

It's a good thing that most of us are aware of that it's important to establish goals. However, the majority of us aren't aware of how to establish SMART goals, i.e. the majority of us don't know how to establish goals and take action to achieve these goals.

The world is filled with individuals who are hardworking but can't achieve anything despite setting goals. The reason for this is open to discussion. But, one of the reasons mentioned frequently is the inability to take a look at what you want from life.

Goal setting for personal development is the method by which you envision your ideal future and discover the drive that pushes you towards your goal of achieving that dream.

What is Goal Setting? is it important?

The process involves selecting the ideal future,

clearly defining the future and assigning your sources (mental and physical energy) for any undertaking which could bring about the best possible future.

Setting goals is the core of every achievement you observe all around you. It's crucial that all successful athletes, business professional, and almost every top performer you've ever met or wish to follow.

Setting goals gives you a broader of your long-term goals and gives you a short-term motivation to work towards the pursuit of your own personal high-performance.

If you have clear goals, it's much easier to evaluate their achievement and their success. If you accomplish a tiny goal, no matter how tiny it is it builds your confidence and drives you to pursue other goals that could create your ideal future.

As I mentioned earlier, the majority of us are aware of the importance of setting smart goals (fortunately).

If you're living in a stagnant state or you're putting off things and putting off goals, set SMART goals that are aimed at achieving exactly the opposite i.e. having a productive life and a fulfilling work. What are the best ways to achieve your goals? Let's take a look.

Chapter 18: Why The Mind Work Like It Does

The previous chapter briefly explained the abilities of the sub-conscious and not capable of, which all originates from the Laws of the Mind on which it works. These rules were created by thousands of hypnotherapy sessions. They are being utilized by hypnotists in order to shed light on the way that the sub-conscious functions.
Laws of Mind Laws of the Mind
Every thought or idea is an physical reaction
As we've mentioned before the sub-conscious mind works according to the idea that the thoughts you make alter your bodily functioning. For instance, if you are worried, scared or feel angry you're likely to suffer negative physical reactions, like ulcers, an rise in adrenaline levels in the blood and an increase in the heart rate. If the idea you are considering is linked with a strong emotion it will certainly be able to reach your subconscious. When the idea becomes accepted, and stored within your subconscious mind, you'll experience the exact same reaction every when the thought or idea is brought back up.

The expectation becomes reality
The expression "I knew this was coming" is never more true that in Laws of the Mind and your subconscious. Keep in mind that your subconscious is working hard to bring into reality your thoughts, which is why negative expectations about your mind detrimental to you. How do you stay positive and positive all the time?

The power of imagination is greater than reason
Ever wondered how criminals commit violent acts because of what they believed or imagined, instead of learning factual information? Now you are aware. Many people let the power of imagination over reason this is why they are prone to opinions, prejudices and beliefs that are based on superstition. So if you are able to take control of or change your imagination, you can transform it into a useful tool.

The opposing ideas can't be held at the same time
A father may be a believer in honesty and might even require his children to be honest throughout the day but still indulge in some sort of dishonesty. Whatever the reason he uses to justify his actions, he'll feel the negative effects of his contradicting beliefs on his brain as well as his nervous system.

An idea that is accepted will be a part of the

fabric until it is changed

The notion that you require an alcohol drink to relax isn't a valid concept However, the effects of alcohol appear to be working because it's an idea that you have accepted as fact. In the meantime, until that the thought is replaced by something that is true or another remains in the subconscious. The longer an idea lingers longer, the more resistance it faces when it is replaced. The symptoms triggered by emotional stress can manifest physical

If they are not treated for over a long period, emotional symptoms could lead to an physical changes. According to the medical experts who are reputable have acknowledged, over 70% of illnesses that humans suffer from result from the malfunction in an organ or other part of the body which were affected by a reaction within your nervous system. What is the reason for the reaction? Sure, it has there is something to do with negative thoughts that are stored in the subconscious. However, this isn't to suggest that anyone who complains about being sick is mentally ill or neurotic however, the mind and the body are so closely connected that the things that disturb one influence the other. If you are still frightened and keep referring to your tension headache for example it will cause a change to be observed in your body, and be visible physically. Once accepted, a self-suggestions will be less resisted by other suggestions.

Have you ever wondered why certain behaviors are difficult to be rid of? Because the same idea has been played on many times, it gets accepted by the subconscious mind. Based on the principles of the subconscious the more time it spends about something, the more difficult to change the belief system, which is why there is difficult time to change the habit. However, the reverse is also true but. In other words, if you make a positive suggestion and then act on it, you'll be able to proceed to more complicated ideas.

To allow the subconscious to react to the subconscious, it must be working less

Experts recommend that when dealing with the subconscious mind, it's recommended to relax. Consider a situation where you're suffering from insomnia or are struggling to go to sleep. The more you attempt to induce sleep by making yourself count sheep and telling yourself you must fall asleep frequently, the more awake you feel. This is because you're making use of your conscious mind, doing a lot to influence your subconscious. However, this area of the brain can't react quickly or efficiently when the conscious is operating at a high rate. Therefore, instead of forcing sleep, let sleep to occur gradually , and without conscious effort.

The link between the Conscious and the Sub-conscious

Based on the final Law of the Mind, it's clear that conscious and sub-conscious minds are connected and function together. There is still a component of the mind that's involved in the equation, and that's the unconscious. A human brain pyramid is comprised of 10 percent conscious, 50-60 sub-conscious and 30% to 40% of the unconscious. However, in this image it is not the case that the sub-conscious occupies the lower part of the pyramid despite being a significant portion of brain's abilities. The unconscious mind is the one that is situated in the bottom section, since it is mostly inaccessible to consciousness. In the analogy of an iceberg, while the conscious mind is what is visible on the surface. The sub-conscious is beneath the water and the unconscious can be found in deep into the dark ocean.

What is their way of working?

The conscious mind is the awareness of all that is

happening around you as well as the present moment.

The sub-conscious mind, also known as the preconscious or Freud described as the preconscious a repository of a wealth of information. It is accessible only when you pay focus on it. The most obvious example is recall of memories.

The unconscious mind contains primitive and instinctual information that's not accessible to the public. Certain memories you develop during the earliest years of your life, for instance, you may not remember them anymore.

How does conscious interact with your subconscious mind?

There are many theories and misperceptions about the role that the mind of conscious is performing. The most precise is based on two essential things it can accomplish, that the unconscious and the sub-conscious cannot do.

Focus your attention

One of the most significant capabilities that an individual has is the capacity to concentrate their attention and focus. If, for instance, you are constantly focusing your thoughts on negative events then you'll soon experience emotions, thoughts and memories that are triggered by those negative feelings. However, if you think about positive, calm and rational thoughts, you'll be able to have a positive outlook on life whatever situation you find yourself in.

Use your imagination

The ability to think of things that aren't real is a result of your conscious mind. It lets you see things that are completely distinctive and brand new. Consider your imagination of being with that one person who you are obsessed with. You'll feel the feelings of love and affection that are a part of your fantasies even if there is nothing happening physically.

In short it, the conscious mind is able to focus attention and to use imagination, both of which are useful in dealing with the subconscious. Why you may think?

The subconscious follows orders.

It is possible to use your conscious mind to provide the sub-conscious direction and the surroundings in which you would like to create. Wasn't it already mentioned that the subconscious doesn't respond to conscious effort? The most important thing to remember is to relax.

With an idea of the relationship between your conscious and sub-conscious mind, it's more easy to control the subconscious part of your brain, utilize the power of it, and utilize it to achieve your goals and goals.

4. HOW VISUALIZATION FACTORS

Knowing how visualization works can help in better visualizing. A technique that is applied without thinking may not produce the desired results.

How It Works

The mind is composed of two parts: the conscious and subconscious mind. The conscious mind is the one that thinks. or rational mind, and whatever that we think over and over again is absorbed by our subconscious mind , or our the creative mind. The subconscious acts similar to an electronic computer. It isn't able to think for itself and it is unable to distinguish between good and bad, or between the truth and the false. It simply accepts, as is whatever is presented to it.

When the conscious mind offers to the unconscious the identical idea repeatedly and over again, it starts to take the thought seriously , and then attempts to bring it to existence.

The experiences we have lived through are stored

in our subconscious mind to where it is able to. It also has access to the Universal mind, where it is conceivable to do anything.

The subconscious is then able to create situations in which our repeated thought manifests itself. I've read a tale that demonstrated how visualization can work in an amazing, but destructive, manner. (So be cautious about of what you ask. You might get it.')

A man had a daughter who suffered from severe arthritis. He tried numerous drugs but had no success. When he met someone and declare, "I'll give my right arm to treat my daughter" Naturally, it was not a joke, however , he did it again and repeatedly.

Unexpectedly, after a couple of years, when he was traveling in a car and was involved in an accident, in which the right hand was severed away from him. Within a couple of days, the arthritis of his daughter was gone!

To understand how visual perception works it is necessary to understand that the most important communication system of our subconscious is images.

While it is able to translate words similarly however, it's much more easily formed by images. This is the reason visualization can be so powerful in helping your subconscious give you what you want.

It's also important to see only the end result, not the entire process. We must tell our subconscious what we want to happen. It is up to the subconscious to determine the method of achieving it.

A picture is worth 1000 words. We've all heard this saying before! It's never been truer than when it comes to the use of visualization. Visualization can be a powerful method to combat illness and disease that you experience in your life. Visualization, which is a method of meditation uses images or pictures to calm the mind and bring our body back to a state of total health. Your brain can be divided into two parts - our left logical side , and our creative side. The majority of our lives are focused on the left, part of the brain that is logical. When we use visualization, we give way to our creative side and attain an equilibrium in the brain. This balance aids in the natural healing process of the body and mind.

Visualization uses images to alter your mood and alter your mood. This alters your feelings that then turn into physical sensations that can alleviate or even eliminate symptoms.

The mental aspect that the brain takes is called emotion, and emotions trigger emotions. The body's physical manifestation is sensation. When we experience emotion, it triggers a feeling that transforms into a physical feeling. Visualization provides positive images to the brain to alter your mood, resulting in an emotion that transforms into a feeling.

This is how you arrive the mind-body connection. In most cases, we're in left, logical brain mode to survive. This creates an imbalance in our brain. In allowing our right brain, we can connect to the mind-body connection that stabilizes the brain. It also allows us to experience renewal and change. It has been proven that negative emotions impede our immune system , and keeps us in a state of mental. Negative emotions slow and hinders us from reaching our goals. It also hinders the brain's ability to achieve the goals we have set. Positive emotions increase the immune system, and makes the brain function in a healthy way, that is conducive to changing.

The process of visualization is simple.

1.) Find a quiet area.
2.) Define your purpose.
3.) Focus on the breath and breath.
4) Start your visualization. Visualization typically

takes a few weeks to develop and needs be performed early in the morning, and later at night prior to bedtime.

Many people experience success after only the first time. In order to achieve success you must be precise when you describe your goals and you can be sure that it's going to be successful! It is true that it's been successful beyond reasonable doubt.

Chapter 19: Over-Thinking Can Be A Numbing

The Life Aspect: Health

The first factor that was found to be directly connected in law Law concerns health. The founder, on an excursion on horseback was able to reduce or eliminate the sensation of pain caused by tuberculosis through altering his mental state. Health is among the most crucial uses of the Law that is why it provide access to healing, but it also opens the way to more advanced uses to the Law.

Situation Problems

In similar to the way our minds are the main source to heal, so it could also be the cause of illness. According to the realm of Law the more you believe in falsehoods or beliefs that are negative the more these false beliefs manifest as illness in one form or in some other way. This is extremely risky because traditional medical treatments only try to treat the illness by treating the symptoms. Only when you're capable of focusing on the truth, is it possible to cure your body by finding the cause of the issue.

One of the main sources of false information getting access to your mind is the tendency to overthink. The mind is an extremely powerful and powerful thing but when it's clouded with excessive amounts of these false beliefs that the body suffers as a result. For instance, if you think too much or fill your thoughts with images of sickness that aren't in fact there, or of ailments that is minor, but considered to be more serious it is easy to attract these thoughts. When you feel fatigued, you feel tired and your body then becomes exhausted. If you believe that you're more sick than you actually are, you actually get sick. This is known as the Law of Attraction, if you let these thoughts enter your mind, they are a real in your body.

Intervention: Meditation

Solution to the issue of false truths is discovered in the very nature of the problem. The law also provides the possibility that when you change or stop thinking about the falsehoods and gain healing. Similar to how when you are feeling exhausted and tired but you also can feel energetic and feel refreshed. This is similar of Phineas his first insight into the effectiveness that is the Law. When he was feeling excited on his horse He was able to avoid feeling discomfort. The answer is to fill your head with thoughts that tackle any health problem you may have or would prefer to stay clear of.

To apply this Law of Attraction, one of the most powerful methods available to your mind to use is meditation. there is no other philosophies that have made use of this method more as much as Buddhism. It is worth noting that the two primary authors of the basic concepts in the New Thought Movement were also the first Buddhist conversions in the West. This is one of the reasons the New Thought Movement although distinct from Buddhism is able to recognize similarities to Buddhism. Meditation is among these similarities.

Meditation is effective because it meditation can not only cleanse your mind of the negative thoughts, but it also helps to fill the mind to achieve the condition you wish to achieve. There are a variety of techniques and styles of meditation that range from the simplest and common, such as sitting on a cross-legged flat area to more complex and extended practice that can last for days is accompanied by a quick. If you're a novice and want to start a simple meditation, this could be a great first step in implementing the Law.

Before you take the meditation posture, make sure you wear comfortable clothes. Take off shoes, belts and tight clothing that may hinder breathing. Although meditation can be performed in the morning, while sitting in the office or performing other pursuits, the majority of novices benefit from finding the quietest place away of distractions or noise. Take a few minutes and ensure you don't have any plans planned for the remainder of the day, to prevent worrying thoughts.

If you're at your best, sit in a seated in a seated position with the legs cross. Set both of your hands over your knees while your palms are facing up. Maintain your back straight in order to let the an optimal lung expansion. Breathing is crucial for achieving the state of meditative. Take a breath through your mouth, then exhale using your lips that are pursed. This can slow your breathing and slows it down and allows you to feel your heart rate slow and help you achieve a more relaxed state.

Allow your mind to wander after it has explored its boundaries and returned fully focused on your mind. Be aware of your breathing, and follow it to keep track of your rising and falling of your chest or the movement out and in of air within your body. Once you are attuned with the beat, start to imagine how air moves through your nose, airways, then to your lungs, and is then carried to the rest of your body via your blood.

As you imagine start to imagine the ways that each organ and cell of your body is filled with vitality and energy. Let it affect you and trust in the healing power which are in you. This process can be used to treat specific ailments. Make a picture of the troubled area in your mindand make use of your power to effect healing in the affected area. Be aware that while you're practicing this exercise, you need to remember that you have to be accompanied by positive thoughts of faith and faith that the body or organ area is liberating itself from the affliction. If you are able to think these thoughts you are not only getting your body back in shape but you also attract well-being and health to those all around you. Be aware that even though the Law can be effective in healing process, you must always consult with your doctor or another medical professional before making your choice of using the Law to improve your health. If you're experiencing an illness and are taking medication to treat it The Law is not designed to replace medications, but to improve the effects of your body. If you are planning to replace your medication with the power of the Law consult advice from your physician.

Transformation: Wellness

When you've applied the meditative practices and techniques, you'll be able to achieve an enlightened mind and body or complete wellness. Always think about the state of health you are in as your body becomes equally healthy as your brain. It is possible to attract health not just through being conscious of your body's health but also by practicing healthy practices. This will result in an euphoric effect, with your mind becoming healthier and your body reviving your mind.

Chapter 20: Practicing Creative Visualization

Anyone can utilize imaginative visualization techniques to reach their goals. Certain people have a difficult time using visualization techniques at first because we don't believe that we can exercise control over our thoughts.

Visualization is an art method that anyone can improve at. Visualization is used by everyone in various ways. There aren't any hidden formulas or difficult exercises. All we have to do is to trust. Creative visualization is a fantastic way to create adventure in your life. It's an effective tool to achieve success and fulfilling dreams, particularly when we regularly practice it when coupled with written goals, plans , and actions that arise from the dream.

Creative visualization includes both active "daydreaming" using our imagination, and active visualization, in which we control what we're creating. The passive is ideal for exploration, wandering playing, and exploration. Many of us can identify with this. The active version requires some time to master, but it is a great choice those who have already got an idea or a goal you want to build practice, practice and finally achieve. If we've got a dream for our lives, then we must think about the details of the vision we wish to achieve, then and then practice it over and over until we feel the sensation as if it's occurring right today.

It is important to engage all of our senses into the imagination. This will allow us to improve our capacity, skills and concentration. Repeated practice will mark our vision as crucial to the RAS (Reticular Activation System) an effective processing of our brain that prioritizes. Once activated, we'll start to recognize opportunities and resources that could aid us in achieving the realization of our vision.

The emotions and feelings are the as the most powerful visualization methods to stimulate thoughts. Innovative visualization techniques make use of our most intimate feelings and emotions to stimulate thoughts.

How do you develop a creativity through visualization and visualization to be successful The ability to effectively visualize and without hesitation is a beneficial skill. Visualization is a component of imagination that can be utilized in the process of ensuring total control over every aspect in our daily lives. However, as mentioned, it can also be utilized effectively to manifest our dreams as well as to heal our self as well as to safeguard ourselves from negative psychic influences and so on.
And, more importantly, these powers can be utilized similarly for the benefit of family members and those who are important to us. The power of imagination is of all creation which happens throughout the Universe and both in the Macrocosm and in the microcosm. All people will utilize these capabilities as a natural part of living in the less dense inside world once we leave this physical realm.
The ability to effectively visualize all of the

beneficial actions requires time put aside, usually each as well as every single day. A minimum of ten minutes per day should suffice to begin However, as we progress by 30 minutes per day, it is much more efficient. Any time that is left over during the day could be utilized to work on creative visualization and other beneficial activities.

Practice creative visualization by practicing these steps.
Every one of us has one particular skill that is innate to us. This talent provides us with a reason to live our life because we love making use of it to help others or to change our lives for the better. In the majority of cases, this talent naturally exists, but it needs to be honed so that we can utilize it better and apply it to make a profitable career for ourselves.

The most common method of improving our skills is to attend colleges or pursue courses in higher education relevant to our abilities. The power of visualization is vital to develop our skills in the workplace beyond the standard methods. It will give us an edge over our rivals. Visualization techniques that are creative and innovative work in helping to improve our mental faculties and increases our confidence. Being confident is another important requirement to be successful.

When we use imaginative visualization techniques and techniques, our brain is placed in a similar state to the state that we actually perform the visualizations. Because our minds play the primary role in controlling our actions, enhancing the process of communication between our body and mind by using visualization techniques can increase the capabilities needed in our professions.

Utilizing the potential of visualization is an excellent tool that can help enhance our skills in the workplace which gives us an edge over others. The key is to practice the techniques of creative visualization prior to and following the actual performance, and practice regularly.

This will assist to improve our professional skills beyond traditional methods.

Here are some steps that will help us practice imaginative visualization to achieve success.

Finding Balance
It's enjoyable to think about positive outcomes for the future. Sometimes, it provides an energy boost however, it's not without its drawbacks. As with all things in life, we have to strike a equilibrium. What is the maximum amount we can imagine? Studies have proven that there are ways to exercise imaginative visualization. If you can imagine the ideal, then you will be able to do it.

The power of creative visualization is immense however, it can't generate results that haven't been earned. Studies show that it is better to concentrate on the practical actions, and not indulge in fantasies that are not real. Imagining positive outcomes does not mean abandoning common sense. The most effective way to imagine success is to imagine yourself putting in the work to reach our goals.

Beware of the Trap
Creative visualization can assist us develop an unambiguous picture of what we wish to achieve. It's most effective when the vision is founded on solid foundations.

Keep in mind that the brain at levels of neuron can't discern the difference between real and fictitious. Making castles out of the air may make it difficult to plan properly due to the fact that it causes us overlook the obstacles. When we create a mental picture of the final result we desire We can be tricked to believe that it has already been accomplished. This is why it is important to be aware of the distinction between seeing positive results and imagining them. The expectation of success as a result of perseverance can inspire us to continue to work. Making hopeless fantasies will stop the essential task from taking place. Through visualization of the right actions, we can transform our hopes into reality.

Making a Plan

The process of creating a strategy can help us get the most out of our practice of visualization. This outline will provide the foundation for effective creative visualization , such as how far we are in the process of achieving our objectives? Did we come up with a strategy to identify actionsable items?

Once we've identified the steps that are required that are required, we can visualize the steps we need to take to complete them. When we spend your time and mentally prepare how to conquer obstacles, we increase the likelihood of being successful.

Focusing on tasks that can be completed you can accomplish several things:
Eliminating self-defeating beliefs
Reinforcing positive behavior
The art of overcoming procrastination

Eliminating negative Thinking

Everyone has concerns. They usually come on the scene when they are not desired. One of the most effective ways to get rid of negativity is to swap them out with positive ones. Keep a visual image of the actions you are planning to do. This will help prevent worrying thoughts from forming.

Designing the Success Model

The cultivation of habits that assist us in reaching our goals can only be achieved through the power of visualization. The most crucial factors in forming new habits and creating positive habits is repetition. The great thing about visualization is that it allows us to concentrate our efforts on building new patterns without anxiety of failing. When we attempt something new, there's a chance we'll fail in the first try. Visualization helps us attempt multiple times to be successful before attempting to implement this in real life.

Another way to think about it is that mental practice lets us perform in the way we want to. When we practice our minds we lay the groundwork for what we want to achieve. We can make corrections when we visualize so that they won't happen on the actual scene.

Resolving Procrastination
There are a variety of factors to consider when working towards the conclusion of a task. If we're not able to overcome our slowness and apprehensions, it can take some effort to determine the right method. If we're worried that our visualisations are too abstract, we can programme our minds to assist us overcome difficulties.

Plan for Visualization Practice Plan for Visualization Practice
Utilizing the right creative visualization techniques will get us to the direction we'd like to go. It's evident that there's an important distinction between visualizing and imagining. Understanding the difference can

assist us in avoiding difficulties while we engage in our daily lives.

www.ingramcontent.com/pod-product-compliance
Lightning Source LLC
Chambersburg PA
CBHW050411120526
44590CB00015B/1921